"*Shipping Performance Management* is a valuable addition to the management literature in shipping and provides a definitive practical guide to the development of managerial shipping performance management systems."

Professor Roar Ådland, *Norwegian School of Economics*

SHIPPING PERFORMANCE MANAGEMENT

LLOYD'S PRACTICAL SHIPPING GUIDES
Series Editor: Peter J. McArthur

Maritime Law
Sixth Edition
Chris Hill

Risk Management in Port Operations,
Logistics and Supply Chain Security
Khalid Bichou, Michel G.H Bell and
Andrew Evans

Port Management and Operations
Third Edition
Professor Patrick M. Alderton

Port Operations
Planning and Logistics
Khalid Bichou

Steel
Carriage by Sea
Fifth Edition
Arthur Sparks

Introduction to Marine Cargo Management
Second Edition
Mark Rowbotham

ISM Code
A Practical Guide to the Legal and Insurance
Implications
Third Edition
Dr Phil Anderson

Corporate Manslaughter in the Maritime and
Aviation Industries
Simon Daniels

Shipbroking and Chartering Practice
Eighth Edition
Evi Plomaritou and Anthony Papadopoulos

Marine Pollution Control
Legal and Managerial Frameworks
Iliana Christodoulou-Varotsi

Break Bulk and Cargo Management
Mark Rowbotham

For more information about this series, please visit: www.routledge.com/Lloyds-Practical-Shipping-Guides/book-series/LPSG

SHIPPING PERFORMANCE MANAGEMENT

PHOTIS M. PANAYIDES

informa law
from Routledge

Designed cover image: © Getty Images

First published 2024
by Informa Law from Routledge
4 Park Square, Milton Park, Abingdon, Oxon OX14 4RN

and by Informa Law from Routledge
605 Third Avenue, New York, NY 10158

Informa Law from Routledge is an imprint of the Taylor & Francis Group, an informa business

© 2024 Photis M. Panayides

The right of Photis M. Panayides to be identified as author of this work has been asserted in accordance with sections 77 and 78 of the Copyright, Designs and Patents Act 1988.

All rights reserved. No part of this book may be reprinted or reproduced or utilised in any form or by any electronic, mechanical, or other means, now known or hereafter invented, including photocopying and recording, or in any information storage or retrieval system, without permission in writing from the publishers.

Trademark notice: Product or corporate names may be trademarks or registered trademarks, and are used only for identification and explanation without intent to infringe.

British Library Cataloguing-in-Publication Data
A catalogue record for this book is available from the British Library

ISBN: 978-1-138-83922-9 (hbk)
ISBN: 978-1-032-59364-7 (pbk)
ISBN: 978-1-315-71784-5 (ebk)

DOI: 10.4324/9781315717845

Typeset in Times New Roman
by Apex CoVantage, LLC

Lloyd's is the registered trade mark of the Society incorporated by the Lloyd's Act 1871 by the name of Lloyd's.

CONTENTS

List of Tables		xv
Preface		xvii
CHAPTER 1	INTRODUCTION	1
CHAPTER 2	PERFORMANCE MANAGEMENT IN SHIPPING	9
CHAPTER 3	DEVELOPING A PERFORMANCE MANAGEMENT SYSTEM	16
CHAPTER 4	MAPPING SHIPPING BUSINESS STRATEGY	25
CHAPTER 5	KEY PERFORMANCE INDICATORS	43
CHAPTER 6	CORPORATE SHIPPING KPIS	53
CHAPTER 7	CASE STUDIES OF MARITIME AND SHIPPING COMPANIES	62
CHAPTER 8	DEPARTMENT PERFORMANCE IN SHIPPING AND TRANSPORTATION	91
CHAPTER 9	IMPLEMENTATION, DATA ANALYTICS AND SHIPPING KPI REPORTING SYSTEMS	124
Index		131

vii

DETAILED CONTENTS

List of Tables	xv
Preface	xvii

CHAPTER 1 INTRODUCTION	1
Introduction	1
Performance measurement and management	1
The need for performance management in shipping	2
Economic and financial performance	3
Environmental performance	4
Operational performance	5
Social and governance	6
Scope and structure of the book	6
Bibliography	7

CHAPTER 2 PERFORMANCE MANAGEMENT IN SHIPPING	9
Introduction	9
The Shipping KPI Standard Project	10
Performance indicators	10
Key performance indicators	10
Shipping Performance Indexes	11
Criticisms of the Shipping KPI Standard	11
The MSA	12
The starting point: Developing goals	12
Financial goals	13
Goals that create customer value	13
Goals to create value through operations	14
Goals for innovation, technology, resources and learning	14
Bibliography	14

CHAPTER 3 DEVELOPING A PERFORMANCE MANAGEMENT SYSTEM 16

Introduction	16
Approaches to executing strategy and measuring performance	16
Financial performance measurement approaches	16
Operations management approaches	17
People and organizational approaches	18
The Balanced Scorecard	19
Implementing the Balanced Scorecard	21
The Balanced Scorecard perspectives	21
Balanced Scorecard objectives	22
Balanced Scorecard measures	22
Balanced Scorecard targets and initiatives	23
Bibliography	23

CHAPTER 4 MAPPING SHIPPING BUSINESS STRATEGY 25

Introduction	25
Strategy	25
Corporate strategy	26
Business strategy	27
Business strategy formulation	28
Company vision	28
Mission and core values	28
The value proposition	29
Strategic goals	30
Scope of strategy maps	31
Mapping of strategic objectives	31
Strategy map development	32
Shipowners' generic strategy map models	33
Shipowners' financial perspective	33
Shipowners' customer perspective	33
Shipowners' internal process perspective	34
Shipowners' learning and growth perspective	34
Ship managers' generic strategy map models	34
Ship manager financial perspective	35
Ship manager customer perspective	35
Ship manager internal process perspective	35
Ship manager learning and growth perspective	35
Identifying goals	36
Bulk logistics goals	36
Container shipping goals	37
Ship operations management goals	38
Technical management goals	39

DETAILED CONTENTS

Crewing goals	39
Chartering and commercial management goals	39
Purchasing and procurement goals	40
Quality and safety management goals	40
Financial management goals	40
Bibliography	41

CHAPTER 5	KEY PERFORMANCE INDICATORS	43
Introduction		43
What are KPIs?		44
KPIs in shipping		44
Types of KPIs		45
KPI selection criteria		46
Steps for creating KPIs		47
Number of KPIs required		48
Frequency of measuring KPIs		49
Differentiating departmental from corporate KPIs		49
Targets for KPIs		50
Improving and changing KPIs		50
Initiatives and action plans		51
Bibliography		51

CHAPTER 6	CORPORATE SHIPPING KPIS	53
Introduction		53
Corporate financial key performance indicators		53
Corporate customer key performance indicators		55
Corporate internal process key performance indicators		58
Corporate learning and growth key performance indicators		59
Bibliography		61

CHAPTER 7	CASE STUDIES OF MARITIME AND SHIPPING COMPANIES	62
Introduction		62
Company A: A dry bulk shipping company		62
Description		62
Vision and mission		62
Strategy goals		63
Strategy and KPIs		64
Company B: A liner shipping company		65
Description		65
Vision and mission		67
Strategy and KPIs		67

DETAILED CONTENTS

Company C: A tanker company	71
Description	71
Vision and mission	71
Strategy and KPIs	72
Company D: Containership charter owner	74
Description	74
Vision and mission	74
Strategy and KPIs	74
Company E: Third-party ship management	78
Description	78
Strategy and KPIs	79
Company F: Logistics service provider	82
Description	82
Vision and mission	83
Strategy and KPIs	83
Company G: Dry bulk shipping company	87
Description	87
Vision and mission	87
Strategy and KPIs	87
Bibliography	89
CHAPTER 8 DEPARTMENT PERFORMANCE IN SHIPPING AND TRANSPORTATION	91
Introduction	91
Typical departments and functions in maritime organizations	91
Developing departmental objectives and KPIs: The cascation process	93
Operations department objectives and KPIs	94
Technical department objectives and KPIs	95
Crewing department objectives and KPIs	97
Chartering department objectives and KPIs	100
Financial goals and KPIs of the chartering department	102
Customer goals of the chartering department	104
Internal process goals of the chartering department	105
Learning, growth, innovation goals and KPIs for chartering	108
Financial management and KPIs	109
Quality and safety management	112
Purchasing and supply department	114
Marketing and business development department	117
Other departments	120
KPIs for transportation and warehousing	121
Performance monitoring in shipping using AIS data	122
Bibliography	123

xii

DETAILED CONTENTS

CHAPTER 9	IMPLEMENTATION, DATA ANALYTICS AND SHIPPING KPI REPORTING SYSTEMS	124
Introduction		124
Implementation of the performance management system		124
Automation and technology		126
Reports and deliverables		128
Conclusion		128
Bibliography		129
Index		131

TABLES

6.1	Goals and KPIs at the Financial Perspective – Corporate Level	54
6.2	Goals and KPIs at the Customer Perspective – Corporate Level	57
6.3	Goals and KPIs at the Internal Process Perspective – Corporate Level	59
6.4	Goals and KPIs at the Learning and Growth Perspective – Corporate Level	60
7.1	Dry Bulk Shipping Company KPIs – Corporate Level	66
7.2	Liner Shipping Company KPIs – Corporate Level	69
7.3	Tanker Shipping Company KPIs – Corporate Level	72
7.4	Container Charter Owner Shipping Company KPIs – Corporate Level	77
7.5	Ship Management Company KPIs – Corporate Level	80
7.6	Global Logistics Service Provider – KPIs – Corporate Level	85
7.7	Dry Bulk Company KPIs – Corporate Level	88
8.1	Operations Department's Goals and KPIs	94
8.2	Sample of Technical Department's Goals and KPIs	96
8.3	Crewing Goals and KPIs for Crew Department	98
8.4	Chartering Department Financial Perspective Goals and KPIs	102
8.5	Chartering Department Customer Perspective Goals and KPIs	106
8.6	Chartering Department Internal Process Perspective Goals and KPIs	108
8.7	Chartering Department Learning and Growth Perspective Goals and KPIs	109
8.8	Examples of KPIs for Accounting and Finance Department	110
8.9	Quality and Safety Department Goals and KPIs	112
8.10	Purchasing Department Goals and KPIs	116
8.11	Marketing Department Goals and KPIs	118
8.12	KPIs for the Transportation and Warehousing Industry	121
9.1	Work Plan for Performance Management System Implementation	125

PREFACE

An intriguing aspect of all walks of life and in particular business life, is the ability to systematically and comprehensively measure, manage and improve performance. Performance measurement, management and improvement are so fundamental to maritime business viability, yet so elusive underscoring a gap between 'what is' in terms of maritime performance knowledge and 'what ought to be'. Probably the lack of the deserved focus is partly due to the dynamic nature of the industry and the speed of developments in so many diverse facets. However, it is exactly for these reasons that performance measurement and management should be at the forefront, not least for incorporating all the aspects, criteria and recommendations being made for ensuring compliance to standards whilst at the same time achieving growth and competitiveness.

This volume which began in earnest several years ago and finally came to fruition, still represents one of the early attempts in a maritime business context to provide an account of relevant background theory and propose specific applied approaches for systematically measuring and managing performance in the business of shipping.

The volume is neither prescriptive nor exhaustive in terms of its content and orientation. It is rather descriptive, explanatory and hopefully motivational in terms of instilling upon managers the need to consider holistic systems for performance measurement and to intrigue students and researchers to learn, apply and extend the boundaries of what is today relevant for shipping performance management.

xvii

CHAPTER 1

Introduction

Introduction

The fulfilment of organizational objectives depends to a large extent on the ability of managers to make informed decisions. This is especially important in shipping which is a dynamic and volatile industry, and the decisions are taken in the context of a demanding external environment of customers, partners, competitors and regulators. It is therefore imperative that in this context shipping companies should develop systems to measure and manage organizational performance, including among others strategic, economic, environmental, social and operational performance.

Companies in the shipping industry are quite diverse in nature. They include companies involved in the investment and operation of ships (shipowners/ship operators), such as tramp or liner shipping operators, charterers who can be either cargo owners or other shipping companies, third-party ship management companies, ship agents, freight forwarders and logistics providers, ports, terminals and warehouse and distribution centre operators, as well as inland transport providers, rail and road operators. Management of these type of companies is required to deal with an array of demands and obligations to facilitate operational efficiency. As such, they need to be able to accurately and systematically gauge and monitor performance as a means of planning, controlling and managing the operations and the business. The diverse but inter-dependent nature of operators in the shipping industry requires the development of holistic and comprehensive performance measurement and management systems.

Performance measurement and management

Performance is the ability to carry out a task or fulfil a promise or claim. Performance measurement is one of the fundamental cornerstones of modern management. Challenges and problems can only be effectively addressed and managed if they can first be identified and measured. If something cannot be measured, then it would be impossible to manage it, control and in consequence improve it.

Performance management includes activities which ensure that goals are consistently being met in an effective and efficient manner. Performance management

DOI: 10.4324/9781315717845-1

1

can focus on the performance of the organization, a department within the organization, or an employee, or even the processes to develop a product or service, as well as its marketing, transportation, storage and distribution. Performance management is also known as a process by which organizations align their physical and human resources and systems to strategic objectives and priorities. Performance management is the fundamental cornerstone of leading a business towards the achievement of its ultimate goals. Performance management involves performance measurement which entails the setting of measurable goals and objectives and is implemented by designing a mechanism for monitoring and controlling the achievement of those goals and objectives within a context of managerial responsibility and accountability. Performance measurement is the process of collecting, analyzing and reporting information regarding the performance of an organization. It can involve studying processes and strategies within organizations to see whether output is in line with what was intended or should have been achieved.

Measurement has been recognized as a crucial element to improve business performance. A system to measure and manage performance should be a balanced and dynamic system that collects, stores, analyzes and disseminates information thus enabling the support of decision-making processes. It is a balanced system because of the need of using different perspectives and measures that when combined provide a holistic view of the organization. On the other hand, the concept of having a dynamic system refers to the need for developing a system that continuously monitors the internal and external context and reviews objectives and priorities.

Performance measurement and performance management practices are common across many sectors of industry. In addition, the measurement and management of business performance is well documented in the relevant literature. During the last 30 years, business performance measurement was studied using many different perspectives which can be principally classified into operations management perspectives, strategic control perspectives and management accounting perspectives.

The development of the Balanced Scorecard concept influenced much of the work and the voluminous literature on performance measurement and management. The essence of this line of research is that organizations need a multitude of different performance measures that will be relevant to their strategic goals and direction and that those measures must be quantifiable to efficiently use them for improving the organization's performance.

The need for performance management in shipping

Performance management is so much more relevant and applicable in shipping for many reasons. The main reasons arise from the characteristics of the shipping industry and in particular the economic characteristics of the shipping markets. Shipping is an industry defined by high levels of physical risk, environmental risk

INTRODUCTION

and market risk which is intensified when coupled with volatility, uncertainty and capital intensity.

Economic and financial performance

The shipping markets are volatile as freight rates undergo marked changes in relatively short periods of time and are subject to the vagaries of the demand for commodities and the supply of shipping capacity respectively. Demand for commodities may change due to changing world economic conditions (e.g. reduction of imports of iron ore by China) or seasonality (less oil consumed during summer months in the Northern hemisphere). Demand and transport patterns may be influenced by events such as the outbreak of the COVID-19 pandemic or the Russian-Ukraine conflict. Supply of shipping capacity is influenced by the decision to build ships in anticipation of growing demand with the implication that the decision will take about 18–36 months to be fulfilled (agreement of contract and completion of a newbuilding project). The aforementioned factors that invariably lead to a volatile market are manifested by the steep rise and fall of freight rates within relatively short periods of time. A marked example are the events of 2008 where, due to the economic crisis the demand for commodities and therefore for shipping capacity dropped significantly with the respective freight rates exhibiting a steep trough. In particular, the Baltic Dry Index (BDI) dropped from a peak of 11,250 index points to less than 1,000 index points in a matter of months. The Russia-Ukraine conflict and the end of the COVID-19 pandemic has influenced shipping supply chains. The creation of backlogs due to the pandemic and the need to fulfil trade needs has resulted in 5-year peak of the BDI registering 5,526 index points in October 2021. The changing geographical nature of the grain trade routes and the evolving geostrategic changes in the energy map (mainly European demand) have resulted in a degree of volatility of prices (e.g. 1,082 BDI index points in August 2022). It follows that a performance management system in shipping should consider market conditions and gauge performance of entities relative to market performance. In addition, volatility itself has been found to affect performance and in particularly fleet growth and size.

Not only are the shipping markets highly volatile, but the extreme vagaries of the market price equilibrium render any attempt to forecast the prices rather futile. Price fluctuations that give rise to shipping cycles may be difficult to forecast; however, it is essential that price related quantitative data are compared against performance objectives to ascertain whether any differences between planned and actual performance can be attributed to the systematic market fluctuations and not to strategies or actions of the company. Uncertainty stems from the inability to forecast the peaks and troughs of the shipping cycles with the result that peaks in trade causes freight rates to increase that may in turn, lead to shortage in shipping capacity and vice versa also influencing investment strategies.

The value of a ship is considerable, therefore the acquisition of a fleet of ships, as required for instance to operate a liner service or to fulfil the transportation requirements of major customers/charterers such as oil majors in the tanker industry or dry bulk traders in the dry cargo industry is extremely capital intensive. Financial performance needs to be closely monitored.

Environmental performance

Several stakeholders place environmental demands on shipping companies including customers, regulators, markets and financiers, and the company directors themselves. Environmental performance is therefore relevant to the contemporary shipping organization and several performance measures have been developed to keep track of environmental performance and to monitor specific metrics that may be required by regulators or the market.

For instance, in the management of tanker ships, key customers such as the oil majors (OCIMF) require companies to abide by the Tanker Management and Self-Assessment (TMSA) standard. The TMSA requires companies to reach layered performance levels and at the same time suggests several key performance indicators for benchmarking and monitoring performance.

International regulations for safety and environmental protection that have been incorporated in international conventions (e.g. IMO's SOLAS Convention) require companies in shipping to develop systems that include measurement and monitoring of performance standards. In 2018, the IMO adopted an initial strategy on the reduction of greenhouse gas emissions from ships. Through the MARPOL pollution prevention treaty, the IMO requires all new ships to adopt the Energy Efficiency Design Index (EEDI) and all ships to have the Ship Energy Efficiency Management Plan (SEEMP). The EEDI estimates grams of CO_2 per transport work (g of CO_2 per tonne-mile). It can be expressed as the ratio of 'environmental cost' divided by 'Benefit for Society'. The EEDI is a function of installed power, the speed of the vessel and the cargo carried. The EEDI should be simple to compute to enable widespread application and adoption. However, at the same time is should enhance the efforts of shipowners in particular to reduce carbon dioxide emissions by reflecting a ship's energy efficiency in actual use. To gauge and ultimate reduce carbon emissions the IMO has adopted the Carbon Intensity Indicator which measures how efficiently a ship transports goods or passengers and is given in grams of CO_2 emitted per cargo-carrying capacity and nautical mile. Every ship is to be given an annual rating ranging from A to E with particular thresholds to be attained. Corrective action needs to be taken for ships that achieve a D or E rating.

To achieve a good EEDI score however, the shipowner needs to develop and implement a SEEMP. The SEEMP provides a practical approach by which maritime companies manage operations and fleet efficiency performance over time using the Energy Efficiency Operational Indicator (EEOI) as a monitoring tool. Implementation of the SEEMP may take the form of vessel speed optimization, route planning, weather route planning, hull cleaning in dry dock, heat recovery approaches and any other methods that contribute to increasing the ship's efficiency and optimize ship operation. The SEEMP needs to be implemented at the ship level which calls for several KPIs at that level so that energy consumption of the vessel can be monitored over time.

Overall the approach of the IMO aims to stimulate continued technical development of all the components influencing the fuel efficiency of a ship. It makes a distinction between the technical and design-based measures of the ship from the operational and commercial ones. It goes without saying that such an approach entails the development and use of not only a performance management system but also relevant key performance indicators for continuous monitoring and improvement.

Operational performance

Shipping is the conveyance of raw materials, intermediate products and finished goods from places of low utility to places of high utility by sea. Ships across all sectors of the industry have evolved over the years with a common characteristic the increase in size. This is because of a key objective in the conveyance of cargoes by sea, viz., the need to achieve economies of scale by carrying as much cargo as possible and thus reduce the cost per unit transported. This is especially true in container logistics where ships sail on fixed liner routes thus keeping operating costs fixed and voyage costs under greater control compared to tramp shipping. Shipping companies operating in maritime logistics supply chains face several challenges in the context of fulfilling intermodal and transmodal goals. They need to measure their ability to overcome challenges and meet stated goals.

Shipping is organized into tramp and liner markets as well as in specialized transportation arrangements. Organization in tramp and liner shipping mainly for bulk and containerized cargoes respectively is a means of improving performance in the transportation of raw materials and semi-finished or finished goods.

The management of ships entails functions that require investment, competency and qualifications and aim at achieving particular performance objectives. Such functions include crewing, technical management, safety and environmental management, purchasing, chartering and operations among others. The performance of such functions, hinges on cost-efficiency and effectiveness, quality, market accessibility and conformance to national and international technical and other standards. It follows that performance measurement, benchmarking and management is of the essence.

Operational performance in contemporary shipping can be measured, gauged and improved through the use of information technology solutions. The collection of continuous and big data from a multitude of aspects of ship operations, storage, analysis, dissemination and use can nowadays be achieved through the available technological solutions. Still, technology itself requires the skill of understanding and management. For example, questions need to be asked such as what aspects to monitor, what data to collect, how to analyze the data, what is a good measure of performance, what is the optimum target, how can the results be analyzed and used? The performance measurement and management system should be capable of providing answers to such questions that stand-alone technology cannot resolve.

Performance in shipping is not uni-dimensional that is performance cannot be accurately gauged merely by looking at one or even a few measures of performance. Not being able to capture the full extent of performance measurement dimensions may actually lead to inaccuracy and misrepresentation of performance and not enable decision makers to undertake the right decisions that will lead to performance improvements.

Social and governance

Contemporary shipping organizations need to uphold standards of social and governance-related performance in order to compete effectively. Social performance considers the relationship of the company with internal and external stakeholders and addresses issues such as employee welfare, diversity, corporate ethics and community-focus. Governance on the other hand, refers to the standards that a company deploys to ensure accurate and transparent methods in business practices be it in accounting, financial, leadership selection, avoidance of conflicts of interest and not taking advantage of insider information and hubris.

Scope and structure of the book

The scope of this book is to provide a comprehensive account of performance management in shipping and the maritime industry relevant to managers in middle and top tiers in the hierarchy, as well as to those aspiring to hone their skills in the art of performance and decision making. The book will benefit most those seeking to understand performance management. It is not highly technical in terms of low-level operational processes for the establishment of performance measurement systems but it seeks to be comprehensive and holistic in the development of an approach for performance management in shipping and maritime organizations.

The book is made up of 8 chapters and it is organized as follows. Following this introductory chapter, Chapter 2 discusses performance management in shipping by first referring to what may be deemed currently as a comprehensive tool for measuring ship operations performance and then making the case for an approach that commences by focusing on the goals of shipping companies. Having goals entails the prerequisite of strategy and strategy setting should be the starting point for any system to measure performance.

Having established the need for a performance management system in shipping companies and the need for developing business strategy, Chapter 3 introduces the concept of strategy and elaborates on various approaches that have been used to execute strategy. The chapter suggests that strategy execution requires a multi-dimensional approach where critical perspectives of a company's strategy should be monitored, measured, benchmarked and reported. In this context the chapter suggests that the Balanced Scorecard may be an applicable approach upon which to base the development and execution of strategy in shipping. The chapter elaborates on the balanced scorecard perspective and explains in detail how the tools may be adopted at corporate level.

Chapter 4 focuses on the mapping of shipping business strategy. The chapter explains how strategy maps can be developed and reviews generic models for strategy map development in shipping. Reference is made to several case studies that cover the entire domain of the shipping and maritime industry including dry bulk, tanker, liner and global freight forwarding and logistics companies.

Chapter 5 discusses in detail the underlying principles for choosing, developing and adopting key performance indicators (KPIs). In particular, reference is made to the criteria for choosing KPIs and the characteristics of the organization's KPI set. The chapter provides a roadmap for the development of the organizational KPI set and for choosing specific KPIs.

Chapter 6 focuses on the development of corporate shipping KPIs. The chapter reviews and analyzes KPIs that can be used at higher corporate level in shipping as a means for monitoring business level strategy. Several relevant KPIs are highlighted and discussed. This is followed by Chapter 7 that provides a comprehensive application of performance management and KPIs through the exposition of several case studies that cover the domain of the maritime and logistics industries.

Once the set of business level KPIs is in place, it is important to develop KPIs at lower levels including departments and teams. This is the focus of Chapter 8 which also analyzes the concept of cascation. Through cascation it is possible to link the higher level corporate KPIs with lower-level department KPIs to achieve the necessary alignment and ensure that strategy can be translated to operational terms and can be implemented.

Chapter 9 provides an account of implementation issues and highlights the importance of automation, business intelligence and software solutions. In terms of implementation the chapter highlights the importance for commitment from the top before a final conclusion.

Bibliography

Bendall, H., and Stent, A. F. (2003). Investment strategies in market uncertainty. *Maritime Policy & Management*, 30(4), pp. 293–303.

Jing, L., Marlow, P. B., and Hui, W. (2008). An analysis of freight rate volatility in dry bulk shipping markets. *Maritime Policy and Management*, 35(3), pp. 237–251.

Kaplan, R. S., and Norton, D. P. (1992). The balanced scorecard: Measures that drive performance. *Harvard Business Review* (January–February), pp. 71–79.

Kaplan, R. S., and Norton, D. P. (1993). Putting the balanced scorecard to work. *Harvard Business Review* (September–October), pp. 134–147.

Kaplan, R. S., and Norton, D. P. (1996). *The Balanced Scorecard: Translating Strategy into Action*. Boston, MA: Harvard Business School Publishing.

Kaplan, R. S., and Norton, D. P. (1996). Linking the balanced scorecard to strategy. *California Management Review* (Fall), pp. 53–79.

Kaplan, R. S., and Norton, D. P. (1996). Using the balanced scorecard as a strategic management system. *Harvard Business Review* (January–February), pp. 75–85.

Kaplan, R. S., and Norton, D. P. (2004). *Strategy Maps: Converting Intangible Assets into Tangile Outcomes*. Boston MA: Harvard Business Review Press.

Lebas, M. J. (1995). Performance measurement and performance management. *International Journal of Production Economics*, 41(1–3), pp. 23–35.

Stopford, M. (2009). *Maritime Economics*, Third Edition. London: Routledge.

Xu, J. J., Yip, T. L., and Marlow, P. B. (2011). The dynamics between freight volatility and fleet size growth in dry bulk shipping markets. *Transportation Research E*, 47(6), pp. 983–999.

CHAPTER 2

Performance management in shipping

Introduction

All sectors of the shipping industry are fiercely competitive and are influenced by the volatile and cyclical nature of the freight markets. As such the measurement and management of performance as well as the striving for performance improvements should be at the forefront of industry stakeholders. Companies need to measure and manage performance as a means of growing and attracting business, for attracting investors and justifying loan and funding/financing proposals, for operational reasons, for reasons of safety and conformance to environmental regulations and for ensuring that they stay in touch with developments in technology and innovation.

Although the measurement of performance in shipping is of utmost importance, there have been few attempts to develop holistic performance measurement systems at an industry level. Performance measurement is therefore a concept that is addressed at an individual company level. One notable exception is the attempt by ship management companies to develop an industry performance management system that would apply across the board of ship operation. Ship management represents the sector of shipping that has for many years attempted to develop measures and processes to gauge and benchmark ship management and operational performance. Such attempts for self-regulation and performance benchmarking include the ISMA Code and later the Shipping KPI Standard project initiated by Intermanager and further developed by BIMCO. The ISM code itself is a regulatory standard that implies several measures of ship management performance as well as the market-based standard for management and self-assessment (MSA) developed and run by the Oil Companies International Marine Forum (OCIMF).

This chapter will provide overviews of the Shipping KPI Standard project and the MSA as tools for developing, measuring and benchmarking ship management and ship operations performance. The chapter suggests that despite the usefulness of such tools at an operational performance management level, the comprehensive measurement of performance requires in addition, addressing other aspects of maritime business performance.

DOI: 10.4324/9781315717845-2

The Shipping KPI Standard Project

The Shipping KPI Standard Project entails the development of a global shipping industry system for defining, measuring and reporting information on operational performance in the management and operation of ships.

The goals of the Shipping KPI Standard Project are to enhance and facilitate the achievement of internal performance improvements in companies that engage in ship operation and at the same time to provide a communication platform between the company and other internal and external stakeholders. The project requires the participation of the companies that will also stand to benefit and requires their input of performance achievements on a standardized set of measures.

The Shipping KPI Standard is developed by measuring 64 Performance Indicators (PIs) that are aggregated to a set of 33 Key Performance Indicators (KPIs) which are in turn hierarchically aggregated to 8 Shipping Performance Indexes (SPIs). The hierarchical structure is linked by a mathematical relationship between PIs, KPIs and SPIs based on data that is collected at the PI level. Performance data of ships is always reported quarterly.

Performance indicators

The data used for the PIs are collected directly at the ship level and the company level and can be used to measure various PIs and KPIs based on the relevant mathematical formulae of the Standard. The PIs are therefore observable indicators, like, number of accidents, number of near misses, number of MARPOL violations, number of dismissed crew etc. PIs can be used in the calculation of several KPIs as many KPIs may be calculated using ratios. So KPIs that reflect safety levels for example may use as a denominator the number of external or internal inspections to find the relation between technical deficiencies recorded and inspections, or human violations recorded per inspection etc.

Key performance indicators

The KPIs are represented by an index with values ranging from 0 which correspond to unacceptable performance and 100 which correspond to exceptional performance. The model measures 33 KPIs. The aim is to measure continuous improvement to facilitate benchmarking internally in the organization but also externally and to incentivize performance improvements. According to the Standard a KPI can be expressed as a KPI Value which is a mathematical combination of relevant performance indicators or a KPI Rating which is an expression of the KPI Value on the scale between 0 and 100. KPI examples include budget performance, drydocking planning performance and ship availability (operational reliability). KPIs will then be combined to a series of SPIs that will reflect performance within specific main areas. KPIs which are chosen for use in the Standard must conform to certain characteristics and requirements. KPIs must be clearly observable and quantifiable measures that reflect valid indicators of performance no matter how many times they are measured (i.e. they must be both reliable and valid). KPIs must be robust against any type of manipulation and non-ambiguous as to the concept being measured. They must not leave room for individual interpretation as to the observable measure and must be easy to understand and verify by different users. The KPI must also be sensitive to change by reflecting actual change in performance over time. It must also be compatible and harmonized with the other measures of performance, and the other variables in the performance measurement systems. They must be easy to use and relevant to the decision-makers and avoid the presentation of contradictory control signals.

Shipping Performance Indexes

Shipping Performance Indexes aim at providing external stakeholders with the opportunity to gauge and benchmark overall performance on the specific areas. SPIs represent aggregated expressions of performance within a particular area and are expressed as a weighted average of relevant KPI Ratings on a scale between 0 and 100. In the KPI Standard SPIs are defined as Environmental Performance, Safety Performance, Security Performance, HR Performance, Technical Performance, Navigational Performance, Operational Performance and Port State Control Performance.

Criticisms of the Shipping KPI Standard

There are several criticisms as to the limitations of the Shipping KPI performance standard. To a certain extent they seem to be justified by the fact that despite its many years of development first by Intermanager and later by BIMCO, the system still stands short of universal acceptability and adoption with only relatively few companies wishing to be part of it. One reason is the fact that companies may not want to part with sensitive performance related information, although arguably this should not present particular problems as the data are not in any way presented in connection to the performance of any particular company. Probably the major issue is the usefulness of the system to the companies. The system should allow ship managers to gauge ship and shipping operations performance against other similar ships and companies with similar operations and that should facilitate performance improvements. The KPI standard is ship oriented since data are collected at the ship level and most KPIs represent performance at the ship operation level. However, there are certain KPIs that gauge performance at the business unit level like for example, retention rate of seafarers or number of cadets on board ships. There are variations in the way data is collected by the companies and also the period of collection and reporting which adds to the complexity and probably defeats the purpose of the system which is comparison and benchmarking. Another issue is that the companies already have good systems for measuring operational performance and therefore any benchmarking standard will not add much value. What would be really interesting and useful for shipping and maritime companies is a method of business performance measurement and management that considers the specific goals, strategies and the environment of the industry and links those to relevant and accurate performance measures and KPIs. This is one of the objectives of this volume i.e. to describe a method, process and KPIs that would enable companies in the shipping industry to gauge and manage business performance and not merely ship, fleet or operations performance.

The MSA

The Management and Self-Assessment (MSA) programme developed by the Oil Companies International Forum (OCIMF) is a tool that aims to assist participating companies to measure their safety management systems against best industry practices. The MSA programme is used in conjunction to SIRE (Ship Inspection programme – Tanker Management and Self-Assessment – TMSA), BIRE (Barge Inspection programme – Tanker Management and Self-Assessment – TMSA), OVID (Offshore Vessel Management Self-Assessment – OVMSA) and MTIS (Marine Terminal Management Self-Assessment – MTMSA).

The TMSA is relevant to tanker operations and provides a framework for self-assessment of safety management based on 13 management practices. They include:

- Maritime security
- Measurement, analysis and improvement
- Energy and environmental management
- Preparation for emergencies and contingency planning
- Management of safety protocols
- Reporting of incidents, corresponding investigations, and analysis
- Management of change and transitions
- Safety Management systems and leadership
- Recruiting and managing shore-based personnel
- Recruiting and managing vessel-based personnel
- Reliability of the vessel and maintenance of critical equipment
- Navigational safety
- Bunkering, tank cleaning, cargo, mooring and anchoring

Within these practices, companies need to develop specific goals based on industry best practices and Key Performance Indicators to gauge and monitor performance.

The starting point: Developing goals

The measurement of performance implies the presence of a core objective or goal whose achievement is critical to the success of the system as a whole and the extent of its success (i.e. performance) needs to be measured. So, performance measurement emanates from the presence of goals (or objectives) in the process of achieving a longer-term strategy for an organization.

In the context of shipping several goals may be identified. Such goals may be broadly classified into:

1. Financial, related to those that aim at creating shareholder value
2. Customer related goals that aim to add value to customers and in extent to the business
3. Operations related goals that aim at improving internal and external process efficiencies
4. Organizational growth goals be it of an environmental, technological, human resource or management effectiveness nature.

Financial goals

Shipping companies operating in a highly capital intensive and volatile market environment need to be able to create shareholder value not least by managing investment decisions through the vagaries of the market cycles. The ability to create shareholder value by buying and selling assets and building and operating assets whilst managing risk must be closely monitored and measured. Companies and managers need to ask:

1. Whether investments are strategically and financially disciplined
2. Whether returns on capital employed are at least on a level par to industry-leading firms
3. Whether the company has superior or sufficient cash-flow
4. Whether the company is operationally excellent

All those are goals of interest to and directly related to the creation of shareholder value.

In addition, decisions as to the timing of investments and return on investments, be it newbuilding, buying second-hand ships or deciding to time charter vis-a-vis voyage charter, charter-in or charter-out are goals that must be monitored. Companies also need to monitor the effectiveness in managing the precarious shipping cycle in relation to achieving their financial goals.

Goals that create customer value

Integral to achievement of corporate goals is the ability to attract, to retain and to create customers through the development of an attractive value proposition and the implementation of customer-related strategy. The challenge to achieve financial goals encompasses the need to achieve customer related goals. In the shipping industry customers no longer focus on core services but rather as in many business-to-business contexts, customers require added value be it in terms of brand, relationships, quality, bottom-line performance and efficiency, as well as cost and price. A company needs to develop customer-related goals and gauge performance against pre-determined standards.

Goals to create value through operations

Integral to the achievement of customer goals are the operations of the company, that could be of an internal and external nature. Internal process operations refer to how well the organization co-ordinates and integrates its internal functions and processes to deliver external value. It may include the integration and coordination of departments, internal communication efficiencies and fulfilment of tasks within time limits.

Companies in transportation need to address various operation related goals including service (how completely the organization responds to customers' needs, wants and requests), assets (how well the organization utilizes, assets, inventory or cash), efficiency (the ability of the organization to keep costs down and achieve economies of scale) and speed (how fast the organization completes processes and tasks and responds to requests). Companies in shipping also need to achieve environmental performance goals, safety-related goals and numerous other operations management goals.

Goals for innovation, technology, resources and learning

No organization can compete without resources, be it of human, financial or technological nature, including the ability to put resources into productive use. Shipping companies need to develop relevant goals for the acquisition, retention and development of human resources, for the development of the ability to innovate and to adopt new ways of performing tasks as well as incorporating innovative technologies. Such goals need to be measurable and must also be monitored. Innovation is identified as one of the main avenues to maintain competitiveness and along maritime logistics chains, innovation is being increasingly recognized as a determinant of success. It is important for company strategies to be aligned to innovation approaches to establish collaborative innovation in maritime supply chains.

The current performance measurement approaches in the maritime and shipping industries focus on operational aspects of ship performance and that is also the approach taken by several of the companies. Operational performance measurement at the ship and team levels is necessary. However, a comprehensive and effective performance management system starts from the top and performance management first and foremost requires the development of company goals based on the company's distinct strategy. Strategy is therefore a key ingredient in performance management.

Bibliography

BIMCO Shipping KPIs. (2018). *The Shipping KPI Standard V3.0*, Released January 1st. www.shipping-kpi.org/.

Bourne, M., Franco, M., and Wilkes, J. (2003). Corporate performance management. *Measuring Business Excellence*, 7(3), pp. 15–21.

Darousos, E. F., Mejia, M. Q., and Visvikis, I. D. (2019). Sustainability, maritime governance, and business performance in a self-regulated shipping industry: A study on the BIMCO shipping KPI standard. In Panayides, Ph. M. (ed) *The Routledge Handbook of Maritime Management*. London: Routledge.

Ferreira, A., and Otley, D. (2009). The design and use of performance management systems: An extended framework for analysis. *Management Accounting Research*, 20, pp. 263–282.

Lebas, M. J. (1995). Performance measurement and performance management. *International Journal of Production Economics*, 41(1–3), pp. 23–35.

Nesheim, D. A., and Fjørtoft, K. E. (2019). Using the BIMCO shipping KPI database to identify costs and benefits of e-navigation solutions. *Journal of Physics: Conference Series, Vol. 1357, International Maritime and Port Technology and Development Conference*, Trondheim Norway.

CHAPTER 3

Developing a performance management system

Introduction

Over the years several models for measuring organizational performance have been developed. All models are characterized by certain advantages as well as disadvantages or limitations so the ultimate goal is to choose an approach that will maximize the potential benefits and limit as much as possible any drawbacks that the performance management system may have. After reviewing the main approaches for the management of performance it seems that the adoption and implementation of the Balanced Scorecard framework can assist in forming a strong underlying model for the measurement and management of business performance in shipping. The Balanced Scorecard is a concept developed in the early 90s by Professors Kaplan and Norton of the Harvard Business School and has undergone considerable refinements and improvements whereas it has been adopted widely especially by successful companies including Fortune 500 companies.

Approaches to executing strategy and measuring performance

There have been several approaches proposed for measuring organizational performance. Many of these approaches are related to financial performance and are derived from accounting and management accounting, whereas there have been a number of operational performance measurement approaches as well as organizational management approaches.

Financial performance measurement approaches

Financial performance management approaches probably represent the most common and traditional approaches to performance measurement. For example, a rather simple approach is Activity-Based Costing (ABC). ABC is a costing methodology that identifies activities in an organization and assigns the cost of each activity with resources to all products and services according to the actual consumption by each. It mainly classifies costs into fixed, variable and overheads and focuses on cost allocation in an operational context.

Activity-Based Costing (ABC) systems seem to be very complicated and very expensive. In addition, several authors have stated that the economical units are

16   DOI: 10.4324/9781315717845-3

in dire need to provide a costing system which collects performance data from the operational and organizational perspectives which is something not available in the Activity-Based Costing (ABC) systems. There have been calls to enhance ABC with Process-Based Costing which allows combination of operational and strategic aspects thus providing an upgrade of Activity-Based Costing (ABC).

Economic Value Added (EVA) is an estimate of the value created in excess of the required return of the company's shareholders, or the net profit less the opportunity cost of the firm's capital. The approach is based on the premise that value is created when the return on the firm's economic capital employed, exceeds the cost of that capital.

Authors have proposed a performance and cost measurement system that integrates EVA criteria with Process-Based Costing and allows the implementation of the EVA management logic at different organizational levels, in the attempt to incorporate strategy into organizational performance measurement.

Another related approach is Shareholder Value Added (SVA) which is a value-based performance measure of what the company is worth to its shareholders. Shareholders prefer that their companies maximize returns, show profits and pay dividends. It is a measure of the incremental value of a business to those who have invested in it. It is calculated by taking net operating profit after tax (NOPAT) and subtracting the cost of capital from the issues of debt and equity, based on the company's weighted average cost of capital. Its popularity was very high during the 1980s but it has diminished since. SVA is preferred by those investors who focus on short term returns that would exceed a market average rather than long-term shareholder value. The SVA model has been criticized for its approach in focusing on short-term shareholder value that may stifle investment for the expansion of business operations or for the creation of customer value and the achievement of customer satisfaction. The SVA approach demotes capital expenditure and as such may not be applicable to an industry like shipping that requires high capital outlays. At the same time the focus is on the creation of cash surpluses from operations that would enable these companies to pay out higher dividends.

Operations management approaches

Operations management focused approaches have been used in the past to assess organizational effectiveness and performance. One limitation of such approaches is that they tend to focus on the operational aspects of firm performance and do not necessarily consider other aspects that may be equally, if not more, important.

For example, the concept of total quality management (TQM) was developed initially to address quality improvements and reduction of waste in the context of a factory production line. TQM has evolved into a concept that entails undertaking organization-wide efforts to install and make permanent a climate where employees continuously improve their ability to provide on demand products and services that customers will find of particular value. In shipping TQM was applied in the business context and manifested in the development and implementation of the

International Safety Management (ISM) Code. The purpose of the International Safety Management (ISM) Code was to provide an international standard for the safe management and operation of ships and for pollution prevention. The ISM Code is relevant to the achievement of total quality related goals in shipping. The Code assigns responsibility to the management of the company pertaining to safety related operations and requires the development of relevant policies and manuals of procedures and processes, the conduct of frequent scheduled audits, regular management reviews, and a designated person ashore to serve as the link between the ships and shore staff and to verify the implementation of the safety management system. In addition, it requires the development of a system for identifying where actual practices do not meet those that are documented and for implementing associated corrective actions.

Project management is another concept that was developed to measure performance against project-related performance indicators. The aim of project management is to achieve the goals within the constraints of time, funding and other factors with the ultimate aim of creating and delivering value. Operations related goals in the context of specific projects (e.g. newbuilding supervision) is to meet specific criteria that are set in the planning phase, and initiate, execute and control the project with the aim of achieving the specific success criteria.

Other relevant techniques used for process improvement include six sigma (6σ) which has been incorporated into business strategy as a means for improving the quality of the output of a process by identifying and removing root causes of defects in both manufacturing as well as business processes. Hence, it uses both quality management principles as well as statistical approaches that aim at achieving specific key performance indicators such as cycle time, costs, and improve customer satisfaction.

Business process reengineering (BPR) is another business management strategy that focuses on the analysis and design of workflows and internal organizational processes. The aim of BPR is the reduction in operational costs and improvement of customer servicing, ultimately leading to the achievement of a competitive advantage. As business processes represent a set of logically related tasks, reengineering focuses on how such processes can be re-designed holistically in order to achieve business outcomes more efficiently.

People and organizational approaches

Following the era of operations and quantitative approaches to operational performance improvements, the measurement of business performance adopted concepts that were based on the improvement of culture and focusing on resources (tangible and intangible) capabilities and competencies of organizations. Such concepts include organizational learning.

Organizational learning is manifested in the ability of the company to facilitate the learning of its members and adapt and transform itself through the process. Empirical results showed that there is a positive and significant association between organizational learning and various aspects of business performance including innovation ability. Organizational learning is also related to the ability of leaders to influence positively organizational outcomes and thus better performance through individual traits, vision, power, behaviour and situational interaction and values. Leadership is the ability of individual managers to guide other individuals, teams or whole organizations towards the achievement of performance related goals. To facilitate successful performance, it is important to understand and accurately measure leadership performance.

Despite the value of the aforementioned approaches to strategy execution and performance measurement it is recognized that they tend to suffer from certain limitations. The main issue with these approaches is that they focus on one dimension of this multi-faceted issue of strategy execution and, strategy is not linked to business operations. In addition, the previously mentioned approaches do not recognize cause and effect relationships among enterprise-wide success factors. An approach that takes a holistic view to strategy execution and performance measurement is the Balanced Scorecard.

The Balanced Scorecard

As previously mentioned, the Balanced Scorecard was first introduced by Professors Kaplan and Norton in a Harvard Business Review publication back in 1992 and is a management tool that provides stakeholders with a comprehensive measure of how the organization is progressing towards the achievement of its strategic goals. There have been other similar in nature concepts like for instance the OKR frameworks which stands for Objectives and Key Results. This framework comprises of the development of key objectives and measurable results to track achievement; however, it stands between balanced scorecard goals and KPIs and is not clearly linked to strategy.

The word balanced tends to indicate and imply a few issues that characterize this approach. The Balanced Scorecard takes a holistic view of performance by highlighting the need to gauge performance from at least four different perspectives viz., the financial or shareholder perspective, the customer perspective, the internal process perspective and the learning and growth or innovation/organizational capacity perspective.

The Balanced Scorecard relies on four perspectives to link short-term activities to long-term objectives. According to Kaplan and Norton it is important to be able to translate the vision, mission and strategic objectives to operational quantitative performance metrics (KPIs). The Balanced Scorecard also achieves its objectives by communicating and linking, business planning, and feedback and learning through a scorecard that helps managers to link strategic goals to actions and KPIs. The Balanced Scorecard consists of a four-perspective framework. The four-perspective framework describes how the business creates shareholder value through enhanced customer relationships driven by excellence in internal processes and focuses on the creation, enhancement and nurturing of underlying resources and capabilities (organizational learning and growth).

The approach is balanced because it uses financial and non-financial measures of performance at strategic, operational and tactical levels. In this context it retains the traditional approach of measuring performance using accounting and financial measures. In addition, it incorporates the perspective of internal business processes that focuses on quality and operational improvements, the customer perspective that facilitates the measurement and improvement of customer related performance and the learning and growth perspective to reflect the value of organizational learning, resources and capabilities for measuring and improving organizational performance.

The Balanced Scorecard approach encourages the use of both lead and lag indicators of performance (KPIs). Traditionally, companies have been using short term financial measures as indicators of performance since they were readily available in the balance sheet, profit and loss and financial statements. It is recognized, however, that accounting measures of performance only provide information on past performance, whereas lead indicators are intermediate measures that report or even drive better future performance. Hence a more balanced approach is achieved by incorporating short term measures as well as measures that could gauge or drive long term success.

The Balanced Scorecard takes a holistic view of performance and links strategy to internal and external communication. This is achieved because companies having valid quantitative indicators of performance at their disposal may choose to share relevant performance outcomes with the market as a means of customer attraction and retention. At the same time, using specific measures of performance can assist in communication to employees as a means of promoting the right behaviours and achieving focused action. The balanced scorecard further facilitates, feedback and learning as well as planning and comprehensive measurement.

Hence maritime organizations may use the Balanced Scorecard for various reasons including:

- To specify, organize and achieve their strategic objectives
- To balance and focus strategic objectives and operational performance measures
- To align customer expectations with delivery
- To align the everyday work of employees with strategy
- To facilitate cross-departmental collaboration
- To track progress towards strategic goals
- To effectively communicate – internally (to employees) and externally (to customers and the market)
- To continually improve

Although at first the use of the Balanced Scorecard was not as widespread, it has grown in popularity over the years and is now adopted extensively in business enterprises, in government and non-government organizations globally. Several management consulting companies such as Gartner Group and Bain & Co suggested that the Balanced Scorecard is among the most widely used performance management tools around the world whilst the tool has been selected by the editors of the Harvard Business Review as one of the most influential business ideas of the past 75 years. The Balanced Scorecard has evolved and is now considered to be a fully integrated strategic management system.

Implementing the Balanced Scorecard

The Balanced Scorecard suggests the adoption of a top-down approach in developing a performance management system. This means that companies need to start implementation of the balanced scorecard by first consulting their vision and mission statements as well as their strategy and strategic goals. This also gives the opportunity to companies to re-consider or even to revise their strategy. Strategic goals are then developed across the four perspectives suggested by the Balanced Scorecard. For each of the objectives there must be at least two or more measures (or KPIs) to ensure validity and reliability of performance measurements. Each KPI has a specific target aligned with the strategy goals of the organization accompanied by initiatives (actions) of how to achieve the targets. The Balanced Scorecard is used to attain objectives, measurements, and initiatives that result from these four primary functions of a business.

The Balanced Scorecard perspectives

The Balanced Scorecard suggests four perspectives upon which to measure business performance. They include the shareholder or financial perspective (sometimes referred to as stewardship when measuring performance of public sector organizations), the customer perspective, the internal process perspective and the learning and growth (organizational learning or innovation) perspective.

The financial perspective is focused on the creation of shareholder value and addresses the financial performance and the development or use of financial resources of the organization.

The customer perspective views organizational performance from the perspective of the customer and focuses on the creation of customer value or the creation of value for other stakeholders that the organization intents to serve.

The internal process perspective views organizational performance in the context of efficient and high-quality internal processes that may include processes for the development or manufacturing of products or services or their distribution through the lenses of quality and efficiency related to the supply chain.

The learning and growth perspective which is also referred to as innovation and growth or organizational capacity views organizational performance by addressing concepts such as the recruitment and development of human capital, infrastructure, technology, culture, management effectiveness and other resources and capabilities that are key to improving performance.

The four perspectives are not exhaustive or exclusive to the application of the Balanced Scorecard. Organizations may actually wish to use more perspectives in accordance with the industry that they operate in and in conjunction to the objectives that they want to achieve. So, for instance, organization in the oil and gas sector have in the past used additional perspectives such as health, safety, quality and environment (HSEQ) since this has been regarded as central to the achievement of the organization's strategy and of at least equal importance to the suggested Balanced Scorecard perspectives. In addition, although the Balanced Scorecard suggests that the financial perspective is followed by the customer perspective which is in turn followed by the internal process and the learning and growth perspectives, this is again adaptable to the circumstances and strategy of the organization. So, if for instance an organization considers its resources as pivotal to customer satisfaction and ultimately financial performance it may use the learning and growth perspective at the top (first) in the hierarchical structure.

The Balanced Scorecard is used to reinforce good behaviours in an organization by first isolating the four separate areas that need to be analysed and then developing goals and performance measures to address those areas. The Balanced Scorecard provides the opportunity to managers to view the company and company strategy as a whole and therefore companies can swiftly identify factors that may hinder performance and develop new strategic changes. Using the Balanced Scorecard organizations can identify the areas which add value to the organization by monitoring the achievement of organizational objectives through the development of strategic initiatives and the setting of quantitative targets.

Balanced Scorecard objectives

Objectives on the Balanced Scorecard are the strategic goals derived from the organization's strategy and correspond to continuous improvement activities that are measurable. Objectives are specific and are relevant to the mission and vision statements and reflect the organization's strategy. Objectives are developed for each of the Balanced Scorecard perspectives and reflect the goals of the organization at the corporate level. However, objectives may be developed at the business unit level and at the departmental level.

Examples of objectives at the corporate level include 'increase revenue' (financial perspective), 'improve customer satisfaction' (customer perspective), 'reduce cycle time' (internal process perspective) and 'dollar investment in new technology' (innovation and learning perspective).

Balanced Scorecard measures

Each objective must be measured quantitatively by at least two measures (also called key performance indicators or KPIs). The measures must reflect fully the objective and must be observable, measurable and simple. A more extensive and comprehensive review of KPIs, their characteristics, development, use and application in the context of performance measurement is provided in Chapter 5 of this book.

Balanced Scorecard targets and initiatives

Every KPI must have a stipulated target which is a numerical benchmark that must be reached to indicate satisfactory performance. Initiatives are documented actions that must be undertaken by members of the organization in order to achieve the targets, meet the objectives and implement strategy. Examples of targets and initiatives as well as how to develop targets are described in Chapter 5 of this book.

Bibliography

Aliakbari Nouri, F., Shafiei Nikabadi, M., and Olfat, L. (2019). Developing the framework of sustainable service supply chain balanced scorecard (SSSC BSC). *International Journal of Productivity and Performance Management*, 68(1), pp. 148–170.

Broadbent, J., and Laughlin, R. (2009). Performance management systems: A conceptual model. *Management Accounting Research*, 20(4), pp. 283–295.

Cooper, R., and Kaplan, R. S. (1991). Profit priorities from activity-based costing. *Harvard Business Review*, 69(3), pp. 130–135.

De Geuser, F., Mooraj, S., and Oyon, D. (2009). Does the balanced scorecard add value? Empirical evidence on its effect on performance. *European Accounting Review*, 18(1), pp. 93–122.

Gunasekaran, A., and Kobu, B. (2002). Modelling and analysis of business process reengineering. *International Journal of Production Research*, 40(11), pp. 2521–2546.

Hackman, R., and Wageman, R. (1995). Total quality management: Empirical, conceptual, and practical issues. *Administrative Science Quarterly*, 40(2), pp. 309–342.

Hegazy, M., Hegazy, K., and Eldeeb, M. (2022). The balanced scorecard: Measures that drive performance evaluation in auditing firms. *Journal of Accounting, Auditing & Finance*, 37(4), pp. 902–927.

Kaplan, R. S., and Anderson, S. R. (2007). *Time-driven Activity-Based Costing: A Simpler and More Powerful Path to Higher Profits*. Boston: Harvard Business School Press.

Kaplan, R. S., and Norton, D. P. (1992). The balanced scorecard: Measures that drive performance. *Harvard Business Review* (January–February), pp. 71–79.

Kaplan, R. S., and Norton, D. P. (1993). Putting the balanced scorecard to work. *Harvard Business Review* (September–October), pp. 134–147.

Kaplan, R. S., and Norton, D. P. (1996). *The Balanced Scorecard: Translating Strategy into Action*. Boston, MA: Harvard Business School Publishing.

Kaplan, R. S., and Norton, D. P. (1996). Linking the balanced scorecard to strategy. *California Management Review* (Fall), pp. 53–79.

Kaplan, R. S., and Norton, D. P. (1996). Using the balanced scorecard as a strategic management system. *Harvard Business Review* (January–February), pp. 75–85.

Kaplan, R. S., and Norton, D. P. (2004). *Strategy Maps: Converting Intangible Assets into Tangible Outcomes*. Boston, MA: Harvard Business Review Press.

Kyriazis, D., and Anastassis, C. (2007). The validity of the economics value added approach: An empirical application. *European Financial Management*, 13(1), pp. 71–100.

Largani, M. S., Kaviani, M., and Abdollahpour, A. (2012). A review of the application of the concept of Shareholder Value Added (SVA) in financial decisions. *Procedia – Social and Behavioral Sciences*, 40, pp. 490–497.

Maestrini, V., Luzzini, D., Maccarrone, P., and Caniato, F. (2017). Supply chain performance measurement systems: A systematic review and research agenda. *International Journal of Production Economics*, 183, pp. 299–315.

Montgomery, D. C., and Woodall, W. H. (2008). An overview of Six Sigma. *International Statistical Review*, 76(3), pp. 329–346.

Neely, A., Gregory, M., and Platts, K. (1995). Performance measurement system design: A literature review and research agenda. *International Journal of Operations and Production Management*, 15(4), pp. 80–116.

Panayides, Ph. M. (2003). Competitive strategies and organizational performance in ship management. *Maritime Policy and Management*, 30(2), pp. 123–140.

Panayides, Ph. M. (2007). The impact of organizational learning on relationship orientation, logistics service effectiveness and performance. *Industrial Marketing Management*, 36(1), pp. 68–80.

Pollack, J. (2007). The changing paradigms of project management. *International Journal of Project Management*, 25(3), pp. 266–274.

Wang, C. L., and Ahmed, P. K. (2003). Organizational leaning: a critical review. *The Learning Organization*, 10(1), pp. 8–17.

CHAPTER 4

Mapping shipping business strategy

Introduction

In implementing performance management, it is important to develop a thorough understanding of what must be measured and managed. Performance management aims at performance improvement and key performance indicators are not developed for their own sake but are developed in the context of measuring specific goals of the organization that drive its strategy and always as part of a comprehensive and workable performance management system.

On this basis a top-down approach is adopted, where the strategy of the company forms the basis for developing the performance management system. On the other hand, a bottom-up approach is one that many companies seem to have been adopting particularly in the shipping industry whereby the concept of performance is narrowly viewed to mean operational performance resulting in the adoption of many operational KPIs without having a particular framework to work with.

The Balanced Scorecard approach adopts the use of strategy mapping that enables classification, understanding and visualization of strategic goals as well as the depiction of inter-relationships between goals and organizational value creation. In its simplest form a strategy map classifies strategy goals into the four Balanced Scorecard perspectives (i.e., shareholder (financial), customer, internal process and learning and growth that includes innovation) and creates cause and effect relationships between them. The causal relations arise from the premise that having efficient human resources, effective management and technology and technological capabilities will enable the organization to improve its internal processes and create customer value and in consequence, shareholder or financial value.

This chapter focuses on the development of strategy maps in shipping and maritime organizations that will enable the design and operationalization of the performance management system.

Strategy

The delimitation of organizational goals requires the setting of strategy. Strategy entails an assessment of where the company is, a statement of where it plans to be

DOI: 10.4324/9781315717845-4

25

at a finite point in the future and a plan of how to get there. Strategy is made up of two Greek words and means leading an army to victory. Companies in the shipping industry have various strategies at both corporate level and business level. Different strategies may be equally effective and companies tend to be revising their strategies more often compared to the past.

Over the last 30 years markets have deregulated and competition intensified. The information technology age has broken up established businesses creating more informed customers and new competitors. At the same time the information needs of the maritime industry have increased, and managers now have more information at their disposal upon which they can base their decision making. However, the shipping business cycles are as volatile and as intensive as ever. Rising commodity prices and political and economic events on a global scale create a continual pressure to reconsider current strategies and to develop new ones.

It is important for maritime companies to develop strategy and continuously monitor its achievement since strategy implementation requires the commitment of scarce resources and provides the feedback necessary for long-term viability. The presence of alternative strategies requires companies to focus and choose, requires managers to engage in informed decision making and requires consistency over time as well as coordinated and aligned actions spanning organizational boundaries. In this context all individual members of the organization need to act in a common strategic direction, hence strategy should provide guidelines, and inspire and empower employees and organization members.

Corporate strategy

Corporate level strategy involves decisions at higher managerial levels that affect the organization's corporate direction and existence. One critical corporate strategy decision is the identification of the business or set of businesses that the company should be in. If the decision is to invest in a number of strategic business units then corporate strategists need to decide how to co-ordinate effectively and efficiently resource flows across the corporate portfolio. Typical corporate level strategies are decisions of merger and acquisition, strategic alliance or joint venture formation, diversification and divestiture and mode of exit (sell-off or spin off). It also includes issues of resource allocation. In a sector affected by sharp and significant peaks and troughs in freight rates as well as volatility of asset values, the ability to effectively develop and implement corporate strategy may lead to sustainable competitive advantages. For example, in the context of mergers and acquisitions it was found that the amalgamation of two or more businesses with complementary resource bases is likely to create operating and financial synergies and efficiency gains, with potential benefits for the involved parties as well as their combined client base. There are numerous examples of such corporate level strategies in the shipping industry. For instance, the decision of pool participants to form a shipping pool and commit a number of ships to the pool is a corporate strategy decision.

Business strategy

Business strategy on the other hand involves strategic decisions and strategies that aim at achieving and maintaining a competitive advantage in product-market domains. It entails decisions pertaining to which markets to serve and which customer segments to target and the adoption of a positioning strategy that will differentiate the company from competitors. It also includes the distribution channels to reach customers, the communication channels to reach the markets as well as the scope and scale of the activities to be performed. For example, a large variety of vessel specifications in a managed fleet enables pool participants to adapt to customers' particular transportation requirements, whether for different types of cargoes, trading in ice, performing special requirements, or any other demanding tasks. A dedicated, safety and customer-oriented post fixture service enhances the advantages of the fleet, focusing on charterers', shippers' and receivers' operational needs. A pool company aims at gaining a competitive advantage by having a variety of vessel specifications to fulfil customer requirements and adapt to customer transportation and post-fixture needs.

Business strategy is about gaining a competitive advantage in the product market domain that can originate by following distinctly different strategies. Consider for example three companies in the tanker business, viz. Teekay, Frontline and Pyxis Tankers. Although all three companies are competing in the oil shipping and transport sector, they have different strategies. Despite the different strategies, the companies are achieving their business objectives.

The business strategy of Teekay is to develop a strong position in many segments across the energy supply chain in order to offer unique possibilities for servicing customers across many segments and increase fleet utilization. It positions itself as the marine midstream company that can deliver services across the entire energy supply chain from the offshore oil rig to the refinery. This unique and strong presence in several segments reduces the risks of cyclicality and enables the company to build a strong fleet that encompasses several ship types ranging from small and medium sized product tankers and offshore storage and support vessels to large oil tankers, LNGs and liquefaction and regasification units.

Frontline's strategy on the other hand is to tap the equity and financial markets by creating a value proposition that would appeal to investors and shareholders. This is achieved by focusing on medium sized tankers to ensure maximization of trading and operating flexibility whilst lowering investor-related risk.

Pyxis Tankers is a Greek shipping company in the tanker business which focuses on shipowning and trading whilst maintaining an active strategy in the sale and purchase markets. The second-hand sale and purchase market is closely monitored and the active involvement of the company during the different phases of the maritime business cycle indicates the execution of a planned sale and purchase strategy. The company recognizes and describes itself in its strategy as an asset player.

The three companies are all in the tanker business but have different strategies. Despite the different strategies all three companies are successful as indicated by their strategic and financial performance results.

Business strategy formulation

Setting strategy requires companies to develop a vision and mission statement and strategic intent in the context of internal and external strategic challenges (environmental, regulatory, competitive) and to define the areas of competitive advantage.

In strategy formulation companies need to consider the key strategic challenges. For example, it may be a downturn in freight rates which inevitably will influence performance. Hence, a strategic goal for a shipping company during a market downturn is unlikely to be increasing profitability bearing in mind the general level of freight rates prevailing at the time.

After considering the key strategic challenges companies need to identify the areas upon which they would focus in order to compete and gain a competitive advantage. This could be strategies of cost or differentiation, that is, strategies where the organization has a core competence of the requisite resources and capabilities that will enable it to perform better than its competitors.

When defining the strategy, it is important for the company to ensure that it will be able to enhance shareholder value in areas such as increase in revenues, reduction in costs, increase in profitability, improvement in productivity, reduce cycle time and enhance customer satisfaction by responding to customers needs, whilst readying itself to capitalize on new opportunities and defend against threats.

Company vision

The starting point for developing a system of performance management in shipping should be the development or consultation of the company's vision. A vision is a long-term aspiration without any measurable goals or timelines. It should answer the basic question regarding the firm's existence. Vision and mission are often considered an essential part of strategic management. The vision of an organization provides a realistic, credible and attractive future aspiration for the organization.

The vision is not the strategy itself; the strategy indicates how a company will strive to achieve (or maintain) its vision. The vision provides an inspirational and aspiring statement as to the destination of the company. Many times, companies in the shipping industry either do not have a vision, or do not use the vision for strategic development.

Mission and core values

The mission is a statement of what the organizations does, who it serves, what matters for success and how the organization intends to create and deliver value to its customers and shareholders. There is a close relationship between the vision and mission. The vision statement is a static statement of what the company wants to achieve, whereas the mission statement is a dynamic process of how the vision will be accomplished. The mission is focusing on what the business is doing today to achieve its vision, and defines the space in which the company will operate.

The mission statement needs to be succinct and may include a rather short time frame (e.g. 1–3 years) and may be further refined based on changing economic circumstances. It is also something that all employees should be able to articulate. The mission statement accompanies the vision and the core values of the organization. Core values indicate how the organization will behave in the process of achieving its vision and mission statements.

Once a company has developed its vision and mission statement, it must indicate how those may be achieved by stating how it will behave in the process through the establishment of its core values. The core values define the organization in terms of the principles and values that the leaders will follow in carrying-out the activities of the company.

Core values may include a focus on new and innovative business ideas, the practice of high ethical standards, and respect to and protection of the environment as well as meeting the changing needs and desires of clients and customers among others.

Statements of vision, mission and core values are important so that everyone involved in the organization, including outside stakeholders, understand what the organization will accomplish and how it will be accomplished.

The value proposition

Following the development of the company's vision and mission statements, the company should consider its value proposition which is a critical link in the company's strategy.

The value proposition is a succinct but compelling and credible statement that clearly indicates the experience that a customer will receive from the company's value-creating offerings. The value proposition is about customers but concerns the organization and articulates the essence of the business by defining exactly what the business will do to address customer needs and to create and deliver customer value. The value proposition can also be used to drive customer communications.

Developing the value proposition requires answers to three key questions:

1. Who is the customer? There must be a clear statement of which customer segments are relevant for targeting and conversely the company may also define who is not in the targeted group of customers.
2. What the organization will offer and do to address customer needs and create value?
3. How the organization intends to deploy resources and which capabilities are relevant to create but also deliver customer value?

The first question requires identification of the customer segments that the organization intends to target. To do so the organization must engage in segmentation and targeting. Market segmentation entails the division and classification of market target groups into homogeneous and approachable subsets based on common underlying factors on criteria such as demographics, needs, priorities, geographic location or even psychographic and behavioural criteria. It is followed by targeting which involves evaluating the attractiveness of the subsets, choosing which subsets to focus on and setting the appropriate strategy to elicit the required results.

The second question concerns the product or service features, value, benefits and price, all of which should be designed to create customer value by satisfying customer needs. The third question requires definition of the resources and capabilities that will be deployed as well as the proprietary systems and processes that will be used to create and deliver customer value.

A value proposition is developed in order to ensure the production and delivery of customer value as well as improving the potential for increased firm profitability. Value that is based on service or functions may not have a long-term sustainable performance impact as competitors are likely to introduce similar features and characteristics. Many times, the greatest value lies in intangible characteristics such as the relationship between the company and its clients, the reputation of the company and the responsiveness of the company coupled with the integrity and trustworthiness of its employees. The performance of the company in meeting commitments and how the company facilitates the buying process are also critical features.

Companies develop specific policies to provide guiding principles to their human resources and employees as well as to indicate to external stakeholders their specific perspective on matters of interest. Shipping companies would normally develop safety, quality and environmental policies. Quality policies would invariably include references to safe, environmentally friendly and efficient transportation.

Strategic goals

The strategic goals of the company establish outcomes in concrete terms and set clear priorities. For example, they may indicate the priority of the organization between growth and profitability. Strategic goals represent milestones in the process of implementing strategy. Examples of business strategy goals are:

- Increase profit margin
- Increase efficiency
- Capture a bigger market share
- Provide better customer service
- Improve employee training
- Reduce carbon emissions

It is important to note that strategic goals represent those aspects of the strategy that are most important to the organization and hence, there should not be too many as there is a risk of losing focus. Goals must be designed so that they are not in contradiction with each other. In addition, one goal must not interfere in the process of achieving another goal.

A goal should meet specific criteria before it can be included in the organization's set. Goals should be understandable, that is goals must be simple enough so that they are understood by those who are directly or indirectly responsible for their achievement. Goals must contribute towards and support the implementation of the strategy of the organization including the achievement of its vision and mission statements. Goals should be communicated to the employees who are responsible for their achievement and employees must understand and accept the goals. A fit or alignment must be achieved between the goals and the values of the organization and its employees. In addition, goals must be flexible, there must be ample opportunity to adapt and change a goal as and when required.

Scope of strategy maps

Mapping company strategy requires the adoption of a top-down approach. The first step would be the identification of the company's mission, vision and strategic goals. As stated already, vision is a future aspiration whereas mission is more specific and addresses the targeted market of the organization and the value added in terms of product or service features and prices and how the company intends to create value for customers and stakeholders. Both the vision and mission statements guide the strategy and strategic goals of an organization. These strategic goals should be relevant to what the organization does and for whom and should also be measurable and quantifiable. The strategy goals are placed on a strategy map which represents the first step in the development of the Balanced Scorecard.

The strategy map represents the perspectives that are appropriate for the organization. The Balanced Scorecard approach suggests the financial perspective, the customer perspective the internal process perspective and the learning and growth perspective. However, it is possible that different organizations may require different or additional perspectives depending on their business outlook and operations. The Balanced Scorecard is a flexible and dynamic tool and although the four perspectives suggested are deemed to be comprehensive in the context of a generic organization and what it represents, there is always opportunity to make additions and alterations.

Mapping of strategic objectives

Companies use strategy as a means for achieving their vision and mission statements. A company may have one or more strategies. Many companies may have simple strategies that at first sight may seem to be similar and straightforward. For example, many shipping or ship operating companies indicate that their strategy is to serve the needs of their customers, to care for the environment, to uphold high safety standards, to remain committed to high service quality, and to focus on the pursuit of technological innovation. If companies choose to run the same race as others (i.e. determine similar strategic goals), they must ensure that they can run that race faster. So, they may introduce variations in their structure and set more ambitious targets in the pursuit of a competitive advantage. Alternatively, companies may choose to run a different race by focusing on those factors that their target market is most interested in and that competitors cannot offer or cannot match. The two approaches have been termed blue and red ocean strategies. Blue ocean is a business strategy focusing on creating new market spaces rather than competing in existing ones. A red ocean is an existing market with many competitors, while a blue ocean is a market yet to be discovered with no competitors.

Companies must ensure that their strategy, however simple, and their business model that includes subtle strategic differences to competitors and ambitious targets and initiatives are the most important determinants of success and performance excellence. This approach will enable the company to survive through low points in the economic cycle and prosper during peaks and will also ensure that it is well positioned for achieving future growth.

A strategic objective turns a goal's general statement of what is to be achieved into a more specific, quantifiable and time-constraint statement. In this context an objective is specific of what will be achieved and by when.

Examples of strategic objectives are:

- Increase the profit margin in the next financial year (target 10%)
- Earn a higher after-tax rate of return on investment during the next fiscal year (target 20%)
- Increase market share over the next three years (target 10%)
- Reduce operating costs over the next two years through improvement in efficiency (target 15%)

Objectives should meet the following criteria:

- They must be measurable. They must address the issues of what specifically will be achieved and when will it be achieved.
- They must be relevant. Does it fit as a measurement for achieving the goal?
- They must be feasible. Is it possible to achieve?
- They must promote commitment. Are people committed to achieving the objective?
- They should have owners. Are the people responsible for achieving the objective included in the objective-setting process? Have they agreed to them?

Strategy map development

Developing a strategy map requires the specification of the company's vision, mission and strategic goals. Identification of the strategic goals will lead to the following step which is the mapping of those goals on the strategy map. A key decision at this point is to specify the perspectives that will be adopted. The Balanced Scorecard suggests four perspectives. As indicated in the previous chapter, they include the shareholder or financial perspective, the customer perspective, the internal business process perspective and the organizational capacity also termed the learning and growth perspective. Although these are the perspectives suggested, they are not cast in stone. A decision must be made as to which perspectives are more appropriate for the organization on a case-by-case basis. The goals must be placed on the strategy map in accordance to the perspectives. The final map must tell the strategy story of the organization whilst safeguarding that it is not excessively complex.

Shipowners' generic strategy map models

Shipowning companies have specific goals that need to be monitored at a high level. Hence, a generic model corporate strategy map for shipowners should reflect those goals that can be classified in the four perspectives of the Balanced Scorecard framework. Hence, a shipowning company may adopt the financial, customer, internal process and learning and growth perspectives.

Shipowners' financial perspective

The achievement of financial goals is dependent to a large extent on the state of the market. When freight rates are high, goals focus on earnings and profits. At low freight rates and weak market conditions goals may change from increase in profit to sustainability of earnings.

In the financial context the shipowners' main objective is return on capital employed and profitability bearing in mind that investments and financial outlays are made. Risk management, cost of capital and cost control as well as revenue generation are goals that may be placed on a strategy map.

Shipowners' customer perspective

In the shipowner's customer perspective, the focus is on what is important to the customers. Under the premise that the shipping company's customers in this context are the charterers, the focus is on those service attributes that are important to the customer including quality such as cargo preservation and reputation and service such as reliability in terms of seaworthiness and timeliness. The goals at this level will also depend on the chartering arrangement (bareboat, time, voyage charter etc). Customers are also interested in the relationship with the service provider, and the ability of the shipping company to provide solutions and be transparent in all business dealings whilst safeguarding the service provider's image (reputation). The question to be answered in identifying goals at this level would be, 'how should our customers' see us for us to achieve our goals'?

Shipowners' internal process perspective

The focus of the internal process perspective is on the goals of high-level processes that managers of the shipping company need to keep track of in order to achieve the company's vision, and mission. These processes may be classified into:

- Asset management
- Client management
- Planning
- Operational excellence
- Innovation
- Risk management

In terms of asset management, the key processes that must be developed include decision-making processes on asset mix and newbuilding versus second-hand investments. Client management involves processes that will ensure client acquisition, client retention and client growth (reflected for instance in the revenue growth from current customers). Planning is about processes to ensure capacity utilization and operational excellence, reflects processes for asset availability (e.g. operational reliability), marine and safety related issues and operational cost control processes. Processes must also be in place for managing innovation which is an important goal in contemporary shipping enterprises. This includes technical innovation, but also financial innovation and innovation in the process of moving goods and commodities in the supply chain. Finally, it is the issue of processes to manage risks, be it market, operational or financial risks which are immensely relevant to the management of shipping companies.

Shipowners' learning and growth perspective

The shipowners' learning and growth perspective entails goals that relate to the management of human capital, informational capital and organizational capital. Hence, high level goals for monitoring the development of human resources, the ability of the organization to grow and learn (learning orientation) are important ingredients for success as reflected in the learning and growth perspective. In addition, the learning and growth perspective should include the ever-important capability of information acquisition and use and the development and deployment of informational resources and communications (infrastructure, transformational applications and relevant software and applications).

Ship managers' generic strategy map models

Ship managers have different goals to shipowning companies and hence a generic strategy map model should reflect those. The generic map for the ship managers is developed as per the Balanced Scorecard.

Ship manager financial perspective

A generic model of the ship managers' financial perspective illustrates the ship management companies' goals. Unlike ship owning, ship management is not a capital-intensive business and hence ship managers will not be so much concerned about return on investment. Instead what is very important for ship managers is revenue, as shareholder value is mainly created through managing a larger fleet and managing under full management (crew and technical management). It follows that goals such as revenue, growth in the number of ships, ability to expand revenue opportunities, as well as cost-reduction and ultimately profit, will define the shareholder perspective in the ship management context.

Ship manager customer perspective

Ship managers offer a service to their customers, the ship owners. The service is related to the conservation of the ship as a revenue earning entity. In this context, it is the scope of the ship management service to preserve the asset, to ensure that the downtime (off-hire) of the asset is minimized and that the running costs of the ship are optimized. Hence, key goals are asset preservation, maintaining ship availability and optimizing running costs. Shipowners are seeking from their manager high quality service (responsiveness, accuracy in transactions, reliability), a good relationship (characterized by transparency and customization) and maintenance of the client's reputation. In addition, ship managers must ensure that cargo is preserved, and that charterers' reputation is maintained.

Ship manager internal process perspective

To achieve the client-related goals, ship management companies have in place internal business processes that lead to the achievement of operational, customer and other development related goals. It includes processes in operations, crewing, technical purchasing, commercial management and risk management. Other relevant processes relate to environmental protection, safety and security. They may also develop innovation related processes to ensure the on-going development of services.

Ship manager learning and growth perspective

Ship managers require human, technological and organizational resources to ensure that customer and shareholder related value is created. Hence, in the learning and growth perspective relevant goals should correspond to the ability of managers to source, develop and allocate resources to productive uses in the ship management organization. Hence, goals relate to the recruitment, development, training, satisfaction and retention of human capital, to the sourcing and deployment of innovative technological resources and to management effectiveness.

Identifying goals

The development of strategy maps follows a structured process that leads to the identification of strategy goals. Goals will be derived from the operational and other objectives of the organization and its departments as well as from the tasks that need to to be fulfilled. The key acitivities in maritime companies include chartering or commercial management, operations and crewing management, technical, quality and safety management, procurement and purchasing, and accounting and financial management. Best practices in these areas together with the vision, mission and strategic directions will derive relevant goals that can be then placed on the strategy map.

Bulk logistics goals

The principles of achieving goals in bulk shipping are similar for both dry and wet bulk commodities. Bulk commodity supply chains are structured in such a way to achieve the performance goals of shippers, receivers as well as those providing the transportation and inventory services. Bulk logistics activities include movements by land and sea as well as storage and cargo handling. Different types of transport vehicles may be used for land transport including lorry, train conveyor and pipeline. Cargo handling activities include loading and discharging and may be implemented using equipment such as cranes, gantry, grab and pneumatic systems for dry bulk whereas pumps and hoses will be used for liquid cargo. Storage includes the use of silos, tanks and warehouses, which represent another aspect where performance must be measured and monitored.

In the context of bulk logistics activities, operators may face particular challenges such as the integration of the different transport modes or even transloading challenges in distribution centres, the accumulation of inventory, congestion, especially in ports, costs and safety and environmental issues among others.

The conveyance of bulk cargo needs to achieve certain goals that must be measured, monitored and improved over time or in the context of company strategy. The conveyance must be timely, low cost, efficient and safe and should add value to the goods being transported but also to the actors involved in the transaction (shipowners, cargo owners/charterers, shippers, consignees, consumers). Bulk shipping must achieve economies of scale and cost reduction through the deployment of optimum ship sizes (bigger achieves scale economies) and the most efficient cargo handling equipment that may be available. It is also important to keep stocks as small as possible to facilitate efficiency and optimization between transportation parcels, inventory and storage performance.

Apart from on-time arrival, departure and timely transportation, performance goals in tramp shipping include the optimization of operating costs (crew, repairs and maintenance, insurance, spares and lubes and administration) the minimization of voyage costs (bunkers, port costs), reduction in ballast voyage distances and costs, and reduction in port time.

Several studies have examined changes in technical specifications of dry bulk carriers and the consequent impact on the economic performance of dry bulk carriers. They have identified that technical changes in speed, deadweight, lightweight and engines for the main types of dry bulk vessels have economic implications measured by costs and revenues. More specifically it was identified that the earnings potential differs between dry bulk carriers with different technical specifications. The relation between technical specifications and earnings potential is direct in that desired earnings potential influences the design specifications, and the specification of the finished ship, determines the earnings potential. Empirical analysis has showed that shipowners also consider cargo carrying capacity, speed and versatility, and other more detailed, design factors. In terms of cargo carrying capacity, a larger cargo parcel enables the generation of more revenues per trip, but generates extra costs due to, for instance, pilotage, port dues, fuel consumption and services. Obviously, a larger cargo parcel requires a larger hull, which will result in a higher newbuilding price. Also, given a standardized ship, the service speed of a ship could be increased by increasing the power of the main engine. This will increase building costs as well as costs for bunkers and lubrication oil. The relationship between speed and fuel consumption is exponential in nature.

Container shipping goals

Container shipping presents many challenges that influence the strategy of liner shipping companies and in turn contributes towards the formulation of their key strategic goals. The main challenges that liner container shipping firms face include market volatility, the supply-demand imbalance and empty container re-positioning, the large swings in demand, cost and pricing objectives, capital intensity and operational challenges that influece efficiency and productivity.

In this context, container liner shipping firms must address financial, customer, operations and learning and growth issues in order to improve their performance.

In the financial perspective a key challenge for liner shipping companies is the capital intensity of the business since investments need to be made on multiple ships in order to operate even on a single route. In this context companies must ensure that performance related goals address the ratio of owning/building versus long-term time chartering of container vessels. Although companies pursue different strategies in this respect it is rather obvious that there must be a balance and that companies should own as well as time charter containerships.

At the corporate level, companies must ensure that pricing is based on the value created to the customer. Hence, a pricing strategy based on value and not on cost can be reflected on the customer as well as the financial perspectives of the strategy map.

In the customer perspective it is important for companies to understand what value means from the customers' point of view, but also to develop relevant profiles of customers and the value they represent to the company. On this basis a company may create specific campaigns and services that are relevant to its target market and capture the high-contributing segments and thus the more valuable (to the company) customers. Sales and return on sales are relevant goals in this context. Customers also require accurate and quick communication and information exchange and the shipping line can certainly benefit from accurate invoicing and increased responsiveness to customer requirements. Ensuring that the 'last mile' customer services are effective is imperative for shipping lines.

One traditional method of pricing for liner shipping companies is marginal cost pricing. Using this method, companies price their services at a margin above the variable cost used to produce it. In general, it is a short-term pricing approach. Sometimes it makes sense to follow the market and price close to marginal cost to fill the ship. Companies also practice yield pricing to ensure that they capture peaks in the market by ensuring that the ships are not full of containers contracted at annual rates which is regarded as low-yielding cargo.

Customers require reliability, responsiveness accuracy on time scheduling, track and trace, added value logistics services as well as door-to-door transportation solutions. Liner companies may charge higher prices to customers that value smooth and reliable transport and the resulting inventory stability.

In terms of the operations perspective, liner shipping companies aim at reducing bunker costs. Relevant goals include the optimization of vessel speeds, hull and propeller cleaning, and faster port/terminal turnarounds that would allow ships to reduce speed at sea. The integration of shipping liner operations in port and intermodal transport activities is also an area that can be used to develop relevant goals. Ports can automate intermodal dispatch of both incoming and outgoing cargo and better integrate planning and IT systems with inland operators. In addition, the management of the sourcing, procurement or purchasing process is important for achieving speed, reliability, quality and optimum cost in terms of fuel and spare parts. Bunker costs can be reduced through a more efficient purchasing process, like for example increasing the number of requests for quotes (RFQs) and better selection and integration with suppliers. In addition, shipping lines may aim at reducing port and terminal costs including the port fees and charges paid for services.

Another area for monitoring, measurement and improvements in liner shipping is the achievement of better asset utilization through optimum stowage. Optimum stowage is achieved by developing metrics of planned and actual stowage, process monitoring of container movements, loading and unloading, digitization of key operational processes, process automation for ocean-freight booking and invoicing and commercial operations performance. A rigorous and consistent performance management system is required to this end.

Ship operations management goals

Ship operations entail the exchange of communication and the provision of detailed instructions and guidelines to vessels, agents, contracts and stevedores on a daily basis. Operations management also involves the planning of the ship's voyage in association with the post-fixture department, arranging for payment of proforma disbursement accounts and cash as requested by the Master, and appointing and liaison with agents and stevedores. In additon operations management entails the provision of instructions for resolutions of problems and claims and the preparation of relevant plans and reports for improving efficiency and productivity in ship operations.

Technical management goals

In technical management the goals are centred around processes to develop and operate an electronic planned maintenance system and create synergies and economies of scale for similar ships under technical management. Goals are to achieve efficient operation of the ship through technical planning and analysis of speed optimization, weather routing, hull monitoring and maintenance, development and implementation of the ship's SEEMP, efficient cargo operation and electric power management. Dedicated teams can be assigned to oversee dry docking and optimize dry docking costs. A comprehensive inspection programme and coating practices will focus on hull maintenance efficiencies.

Crewing goals

Crewing practices include the efficient recruitment and management of crew. In terms of crew recruitment, companies must ensure improvement in crew access and speed of recruitment through marine academies and a cadetship programme. The recruited crew must be of high quality in terms of qualifications, skills and competencies and must have passed relevant medical tests. It is preferable to have a common language, therefore proficiency in English is important. In terms of crew management, companies may focus on training and crew development and the use of technology for this purpose (e.g. bridge and engine simulators), crew remuneration and leave packages, crew welfare practices and quality of work environment (communication, internet on board), improvement of crew information quality and use of integrated electronic software crew management systems.

Chartering and commercial management goals

Chartering or commercial management is a key function for shipping companies as it entails the ability to find appropriate employment for the ships that includes the ability to negotiate short term and long term charters and to deploy the ships effectively, and fully implementing the requirements of the charterparties. Goals include the maximization of profits per charter, chartering effectiveness i.e. the percentage of time charters fulfilled without problems, or in the case of voyage charters the number of times that the ship has not arrived on time, the number of times that notice of readiness (NOR) has been issued on-time, late or turned down, chartering productivity which may include time charters contribution to profit or revenue, voyage costs/bunker fuel optimization, time charter speed and consumption deviations, time charter on-time delivery, and voyage charter productivity that may be reflected in the number of positions per time period.

Purchasing and procurement goals

Contempoary purchasing and procurement best practices make use of a centralized electronic purchasing system and a simplified process by which the company and its suppliers communicate electronically. Products are usually classified into electrical equipment, safety equipment, consumables etc. This also enables the planning for fleet-wide procurement and the use of strategic sourcing activities which include identification of suppliers, development of supplier relationships and having a structured purchasing process with specialized dedicated expert personnel that makes use of electronic databases and marketplaces.

Quality and safety management goals

In terms of the quality and safety management tasks of the organization, goals relate to the achievement of relevant certification for maritime and non-maritime quality standards like for instance, ISO14001 Environmental Management System, ISO5001 Energy Management System, BS OHSAS 18001 Occupational Health and Safety Standard as well as the ISM Code and other relevant market standards (e.g. TMSA). It also includes measures to improve health and safety on board vessels and training of crew for health and safety related matters. It is also important to adopt electronic systems for quality, safety, health and the environment.

Financial management goals

Financial management entails a harmonized accounting system that integrates accounting, financial management as well as other cost-related aspects such as purchasing and cash management procedures. In terms of the cash management procedures it is important not to rely on past accounting data but to invest in real time short term cash forecast and active cash management procedures combining real time cash, credits and debits. Cash budgeting should inlcude receivables and payables in the context of a period-related schedule.

Budgets must be developed to cover the key operations and activities such as a crewing budget, an operational budget, a materials/spares part budget, and an information technology budget among others. Best practices entail the comparison of actual and budgeted estimation and transactions as a means for planning for future improvements in budgeting and cash management. A master budget may serve as a planning and control tool for management, enabling managers to plan their business activities during one-year periods.

Bibliography

Ahn, H. (2005). How to individualise your balanced scorecard? *Measuring Business Excellence*, 9(1), pp. 5–12.

Alexandridis, G., Antypas, N., Gulnur, A., and Visvikis, I. (2020). Corporate financial leverage and M&As choices: Evidence from the shipping industry. *Transportation Research Part E: Logistics and Transportation Review*, 133.

Alexandrou, G., Gounopoulos, D., and Hardy, M. T. (2014). Mergers and acquisitions in shipping. *Transportation Research Part E: Logistics and Transportation Review*, 61, pp. 212–234.

Cokins, G. (2020). The strategy map and its balanced scorecard. *EDPACS*, 61(3), pp. 1–16.

Direction, S. (2021). Not just the bottom line: Using balance scorecard strategies to broaden organizational success metrics. *Strategic Direction*, 37(3), pp. 7–8.

Drobetz, W., Gavriilidis, K., Krokida, S.-I., and Tsouknidis, D. (2021). The effects of geopolitical risk and economic policy uncertainty on dry bulk shipping freight rates. *Applied Economics*, 53(19), pp. 2218–2229

Goldstein, J. C. (2022). Strategy maps: The middle management perspective. *Journal of Business Strategy*, 43(1), pp. 3–9.

Gomes, J., and Romao, M. (2017). Balanced scorecard: Today's challenges. *Advances in Intelligent Systems and Computing*, 569(1), pp. 257–266.

Haralambides, H. E. (2019). Gigantism in container shipping, ports and global logistics: A time-lapse into the future. *Maritime Economics and Logistics*, 21, pp. 1–60.

Hu, B., Leopold-Wildburger, U., and Strohhecker, J. (2017). Strategy map concepts in a balanced scorecard cockpit improve performance. *European Journal of Operational Research*, 258(2), pp. 664–676.

Kaplan, R. S. (2009). Conceptual foundations of the balanced scorecard. *Handbooks of Management Accounting Research*, 3, pp. 1253–1269.

Kaplan, R. S., and Norton, D. P. (1996). Linking the balanced scorecard to strategy. *California Management Review*, 39(1), pp. 53–79.

Kaplan, R. S., and Norton, D. P. (2000). Having trouble with your strategy? Then map it. *Focusing Your Organization on Strategy – With the Balanced Scorecard*, 49(5), pp. 167–176.

Kaplan, R. S., and Norton, D. P. (2004). *Strategy Maps: Converting Intangible Assets into Tangible Outcomes*. Boston, MA: Harvard Business Review Press.

Kaplan, R. S., and Norton, D. P. (2004). The strategy map: Guide to aligning intangible assets. *Strategy & Leadership*, 32(5), pp. 10–17.

Kaplan, R. S., and Norton, D. P. (2005). *The Balanced Scorecard: Measures that Drive Performance* (Vol. 70, pp. 71–79). Boston, MA: Harvard Business Review Press.

Kim, W. C., and Mauborgne, R. (2005). *Blue Ocean Strategy: How to Create Uncontested Market Space and Make Competition Irrelevant*. Boston, MA: Harvard Business Review Press.

Kun, K. H., Khim, K., and Webb, A. (2022). Strategy maps in changing times. *Strategic Finance*, 104(4), pp. 23–24.

Lawrie, G., and Cobbold, I. (2004). Third-generation balanced scorecard: Evolution of an effective strategic control tool. *International Journal of Productivity and Performance Management*, 53(7), pp. 611–623.

Markiewicz, P. (2013). Methodical aspects of applying strategy map in an organization. *Business, Management and Economics Engineering*, 11(1), pp. 153–167.

Marr, B., and Adams, C. (2004). The balanced scorecard and intangible assets: Similar ideas, unaligned concepts. *Measuring Business Excellence*, 8(3), pp. 18–27.

Mehralian, G., Nazari, J. A., Nooriparto, G., and Rasekh, H. R. (2017). TQM and organizational performance using the balanced scorecard approach. *International Journal of Productivity and Performance Management*, 66(1), pp. 111–125.

Sundin, H., Granlund, M., and Brown, D. A. (2010). Balancing multiple competing objectives with a balanced scorecard. *European Accounting Review*, 19(2), pp. 203–246.

Tapinos, E., Dyson, R. G., and Meadows, M. (2011). Does the balanced scorecard make a difference to the strategy development process? *Journal of the Operational Research Society*, 62(5), pp. 888–899.

Trapp, A. C., Harris, I., Rodrigues, V. S., and Sarkis, J. (2020). Maritime container shipping: Does coopetition improve cost and environmental efficiencies? *Transportation Research Part D: Transport and Environment*, 87.

Wu, X., Zhang, L., and Luo, M. (2020). Current strategic planning for sustainability in international shipping. *Environmental Development and Sustainability*, 22, pp. 1729–1747.

CHAPTER 5

Key performance indicators

Introduction

Managers need to continuously analyze and improve the efficiency and effectiveness of their business strategies. To accomplish this, they must focus on achieving the alignment of strategies, business goals, metrics and initiatives. This entails the creation of a framework that will enable the monitoring of business performance and allow reporting of results through the utilization of dashboards and automation solutions that will facilitate management of business performance.

The adoption of key performance indicators (KPIs) has been very prominent in the shipping industry over the last decade or so. Companies have readily embarked on a drive to enhance their performance management system by considering and selecting relevant KPIs. In the shipping industry, companies mainly use KPIs that reflect operational performance, so it is important to enhance the performance management system by considering KPIs that measure financial and general business performance. KPIs should be linked to the company's strategy and should provide feedback on whether the strategic direction is followed and whether strategy goals are met.

Companies include key performance indicators in their annual and corporate reports as a means of enabling current and potential customers and partners to assess company strategies and evaluate the potential for success. It is therefore essential that KPIs are always linked to strategies and strategic goals, in order to gain the level of understanding required.

It is also critical to choose the right KPIs and have a balanced set that reflects comprehensively all aspects of operational and business performance. In addition, KPIs have certain characteristics that may indicate their use for the achievement of specific purposes. For example, some KPIs may report historical performance, whereas others may drive future performance. On this basis the choice of the KPI set to be adopted is of fundamental importance.

This chapter reviews the current situation with respect to the adoption of KPIs in shipping and provides a discussion of the criteria for choosing and developing a balanced set of KPIs as a means of constructing an effective performance management system.

DOI: 10.4324/9781315717845-5

What are KPIs?

According to the United Kingdom's Companies Act (2006) section 417(6) 'Key performance indicators' means factors by reference to which the development, performance or position of the business of the company can be measured effectively. KPIs are concise statements that describe the specific things an organization must perform well to ensure that it is on the right course for implementing its strategy successfully. It is a measurable value, demonstrating the effectiveness of achieving key business objectives.

KPIs are defined as quantifiable or qualitative measures that enable organizations to gauge their effectiveness in achieving strategic and operational goals. KPIs provide insight into whether an organization is achieving its objectives and they foster accountability for results. In this context there should be a system that provides the basis for reporting a balanced and comprehensive set of KPIs that reflects an accurate view of the achievement of business objectives and facilitates decision making.

Organizations may use KPIs at various levels such as at corporate level, as part of an actionable scorecard, or to evaluate reaching targets of overall enterprise performance. KPIs are used by executives to evaluate business performance and determine whether they are adhering to the strategic plan. They are also used at department level to evaluate reaching targets in operations, chartering and other lower-level internal business processes. By using KPIs for performance measurement, managers are able to evaluate business goals against pre-determined benchmarks. This allows variations in performance to be immediately visualized and if results fall below a set standard to take immediate action and achieve quick rectification. When a KPI shows that performance is consistently meeting or exceeding the required level, managers may decide to raise the bar and set a higher standard to aspire to. For this reason, KPIs are essential for any business improvement strategy.

KPIs in shipping

Maritime companies do employ KPIs to manage performance. However, for many companies the set of KPIs is characterized by certain distinct limitations. Firstly, the KPI set is many times over-reliant on accounting performance metrics such as profit, loss and other balanced sheet or financial statement measures. This may be so, because such measures need to be recorded by the companies as part of their obligations to abide by international accounting standards and local and international legislation and also because such measures are readily available and easy to retrieve, record and report. In addition, many KPI sets contain measures that focus on operational aspects of the company and tend to ignore key business-related aspects. So, in a KPI set for a company in shipping one may expect to find measures reflecting emissions (such as Sox, Nox), operational safety (such as Loss Time Injury Frequency, LTIF), which despite their importance and relevance are measures of an operational nature that are more applicable when measuring performance at a lower department level rather than of a corporation.

If companies predominantly employ accounting and operational KPIs for managing performance, there is a need to develop a systematic and comprehensive performance management system that would focus on measuring, analyzing and managing performance to achieve strategic goals, maximize effectiveness and optimize the return on investment. Companies must ensure that they have the right KPIs, that the KPI set is balanced (i.e. not over-reliant on accounting or operational measures) and that the KPI set is aligned to industry KPIs. It is also important to ensure that the KPI set promotes the right behaviour among organizational members.

KPIs must be used by management to manage performance by implementing several actions. KPIs must be reported and discussed at different managerial levels and must facilitate decision making and actions at these levels. It is important to have a clear understanding of cascading KPIs to lower levels, of establishing supporting processes and of investing in automation solutions that will facilitate the implementation of the performance management system. In effect, KPIs should help the company implement their strategy.

Types of KPIs

For each objective on the strategy map, at least two measures (KPIs) need to be identified and tracked over time. KPIs indicate progress toward a desirable outcome. Strategic KPIs monitor the implementation and effectiveness of an organization's strategies. KPIs also aim to determine the gap between actual and targeted performance and determine organization effectiveness and operational efficiency.

KPIs can be of several types and their effectiveness hinges to a large extent on the use of the appropriate KPI for the measurement of a specific goal in the context that an organization wants to measure it. There are different KPIs and the choice may be based on the specific standards of the industry leading to a set of homogeneous measures. However, setting indicators only on the basis of industry standards without considering business needs can lead to failure since companies have different strategies and KPIs should ultimately measure the strategic direction of the companies. Managers should not feel compelled to create KPIs to match those adopted or used and reported by companies in their industry or sector. The overriding need is for the KPIs to be relevant to that particular company.

Most KPIs are quantitative in that results are numerical in nature. The most common KPIs used by companies are financial indicators and these are quantitative indicators and may be derived from accounting standards and ratios. However, companies may also use qualitative indicators that may not be presentable numerically. Companies may also use the so called leading and lagging indicators of performance. Leading indicators are those that can predict the outcome of a process and even drive that outcome. They measure intermediate processes and activities and are more difficult to capture. Examples include 'hours spent with customers' or 'number of proposals written' or 'number of quotations to prospects'. They are predictive in nature and allow organizations to adjust during the process. Lagging indicators are those that measure the success or failure after the completion of a process or action. These indicators focus on the results at the end of a time period like accounting profit and loss measures. They represent past performance and are easier to retrieve and use and are therefore more commonly used by organizations. They are historical in nature and therefore lack predictive power. Examples include 'market share', 'sales' and 'employee satisfaction'.

Input indicators are those that measure the number of resources that are used during the production process or during the generation of an outcome. 'Dollars invested' or 'number of employees in a particular project or process' or 'number of cranes deployed' or 'number of square metres of warehouse' are all examples of input KPIs. Output indicators reflect the outcome or results of the activities that have taken place during the process. Financial measures are output measures of performance, so is 'customer satisfaction', or 'on-time delivery'. On the other hand, process indicators represent the efficiency or productivity of the process.

KPI selection criteria

Different objectives of the system (organization) mean different aspects of production need to be measured. At different managerial levels, the indicators should be different. Given the complexity and multi-facet nature of the business of shipping, multiple indicators are normally used. To measure supply chain performance, financial and non-financial performance should be considered. Authors suggest the use of service, operational and financial metrics, which have to be selected according to the strategic objectives of the retailer.

There are certain rules that if followed will lead to a selection of an appropriate set of KPIs. It is generally believed that the more KPIs the better it would be for gauging performance. However, it is preferable for companies to begin with a small number of KPIs. These KPIs should adhere to the first criterion that is, a choice of KPIs that are necessary for achieving the goals of the organization. In addition, it would be a reasonably small set so that they can be successfully managed at the corporate level.

In choosing KPIs companies should not overcomplicate the measurement decision. Although, new and missing measures are valuable, many times the most obvious measure that comes to mind is also the most appropriate. Another criterion is that KPIs must be made up of a mix of lead and lag indicators as explained previously. Companies must ensure that KPIs are quantifiable, that is they can be measured precisely, and organizations should be able to verify them at a later stage. KPIs should be valid and reliable, based on credible and accurate data and should be easy to calculate and understand. For instance, one of the challenges of companies in the shipping industry with current industry standards has been that many KPIs are based on rather advanced mathematical formulae that may not be so easy and simple to understand and use. KPIs should be timely and comparable. In other words, the retrieved data need to be available to be used and reported within a useful timeframe but should also be used to make comparisons with other data that are collected over time. Finally, the collection, retrieval and/ or capture of data should not cost too much in time and resources. It is important that all indicators are practical and reflect and integrate with existing company processes whilst specifying whether or not the company is actually improving, i.e. they are directional and can be used by the organization to control and effect change (actionable KPIs).

The set of KPIs should be meaningful, that is related significantly and directly to an organization's vision, mission and goals, it should be valuable i.e. measure the most important activities of the organization, it should be balanced that is inclusive of several types of measures (i.e., quality, efficiency) and linked or matched to a unit responsible for achieving the targeted measure.

On this basis a set of effective KPIs should:

- Provide an objective way to establish that the company's strategy is effectively implemented. This can be achieved by adopting a top-down approach with strategy being the starting point
- Provide the basis for monitoring performance and performance changes over time
- Focus employee attention, actions and behaviours on the aspects that are most critical for organizational success
- Measure intermediate processes (using lead KPIs) as well as end results (with lag KPIs)
- Enable internal communication to employees as well as external communication to customers and stakeholders
- Facilitate reduction of risk and uncertainty.

Steps for creating KPIs

The first step in creating KPIs is to identify their scope and purpose. On this basis, the company must establish what needs to be measured, i.e. specify the strategic goals. Every company must evaluate and assess the areas for developing KPIs that would reflect and measure its own goals and performance. There are different objectives in the organizational system which are idiosyncratic, which means that different aspects of service, production and organizational performance need to be measured. This determination is critical for process improvement, organizational effectiveness, and for ensuring profitability. At different managerial levels, the indicators should be different and managers should aim at identifying KPIs that are relevant to the business needs but at their own level. Given the complexity and multitude of areas and contexts of shipping company operations, multiple indicators are normally used.

Prior to the selection of any KPI, there must be a due diligence process to assess the relevance, purpose and usefulness of each indicator as a measure of the predetermined goal as well as to determine the fit or alignment of the indicator to that goal. Since KPIs are measures of critical organizational success factors and goals, the KPIs will be essential for monitoring and controlling the goals that have an impact on the organization's bottom line.

When developing KPIs, the focus is on critical organizational activities and the following parameters should be considered:

- Number of KPIs to be formulated
- Identifying the purpose for establishing each KPI
- Whether or not there is need for KPIs at all organizational levels
- KPIs manageability and controllability
- Differentiating departmental from enterprise wide KPIs
- Frequency of measuring KPIs
- Targets to be set for the identified KPIs
- Infrastructure to support the formulated KPIs.

All the points should be addressed in detail for creating insightful and effective indicators.

Number of KPIs required

This is one of the most common questions that arise and concerns the number of KPIs that are required to accurately and precisely measure and reflect the stated business goals. The answer to this question lies in understanding that key performance indicators should be set only for the critical success goals and that for each goal there must approximately two to three KPIs. Multiple metrics are needed, although some occasionally single metrics may be used to express certain types of performance such as financial performance. Many managers wrongly believe that taking an all-encompassing approach of building as many indicators as they can, will lead to better results. However, having too many KPIs can lead to difficulty or even inability to manage the measurement process and defeat the purpose for which the system was developed in the first place, that is to enhance and simplify decision making. Any information overload will hinder managers from identifying and using the right information as and when they need it. It will also make it very difficult to develop a streamlined measurement scorecard with causal linkages. To facilitate the development process KPIs may be classified in relation to the performance goal being measured such as cost, quality, delivery, safety, etc. The classification will be based on the nature of the business and its strategic goals.

It is valuable to measure goals with more than one indicator as studies have shown that using subjective measures of performance without triangulating the results with objectively measurable KPIs and from different data sources where possible, may lead to inaccurate performance measurements.

Frequency of measuring KPIs

To assess whether critical business objectives can be met, it is essential for performance indicators to be regularly monitored. This is the case for KPIs at all levels, be it at a higher corporate level where indicators such as sales, sales growth, cost and risk will be monitored but also at lower levels where customer satisfaction, reliability, quality and cost need to be tracked. The period for measuring indicators, determined by management, can be daily, monthly, quarterly or annually. There are instances where operational KPIs may be measured even on an hourly rate. Daily measures may also assist managers in improving team performance and instil a culture of continuous improvement. However, one must consider very carefully whether measuring KPIs daily or less will be useful bearing in mind the volatility that such measures may undergo and the impact on employee behaviour who may lead to unorthodox focus on short term improvements. Many times, any real process improvements will not take effect for weeks or months, hence daily measurements will not be very effective.

It is very important for companies to identify and establish the frequency of measuring KPIs as well as the period over which the KPI is measured and reported. Performance monitoring may take place over closed periods (e.g. at the end of a specified period such as at the end of the financial year), over open periods (e.g. year to date reporting that do not provide means for comparisons over time) and over moving periods (e.g. monthly or quarterly). The latter provide better and more accurate measurements as they are comparably shorter periods and do not suffer from high volatility risk.

Differentiating departmental from corporate KPIs

A holistic performance management system requires the development of KPIs at different levels. It is therefore important for departments and teams to establish KPIs in order to measure performance within their respective areas. KPIs at all levels should be linked and focused on achieving the strategic goals at corporate level. This means that the workforce is strategy focused and KPIs at the group or real level will often roll up to the organizational level ensuring that everyone is working towards the achievement of the strategic goals of the organization. This is called alignment of employee goals at different levels to corporate level goals and objectives. To this end, performance indicators are often needed at the individual and team levels in addition to organizational levels. In addition, employees at all levels are responsible and are often held accountable for meeting various targets set by senior management.

A challenge faced by organizations and individuals involved in the selection and development of KPIs is whether the corporate KPI set are relevant to the corporate balanced scorecard, i.e. whether it would allow the top managers to assess progress against the stated mission, vision and strategic objectives. If this is the case, then these are regarded as corporate KPIs. However, if the KPIs are not corporate KPIs, then those should be considered as part of the measurement system for business units or departments at a lower level.

To distinguish between corporate and departmental KPIs but also establish a relation between them, the Balanced Scorecard framework suggests the adoption of the cascation approach. Through cascation the company benefits by having the KPIs chosen for the corporate and departmental scorecards to be layered or to be hierarchically organized.

If KPIs are hierarchically grouped as top-tier, middle-tier and low-tier it enables top managers to follow through and identify the root causes of under-performance at lower levels. The lower-level metrics are therefore designed to reveal the reasons behind under-performance. The different levels of metrics are relevant to different managerial levels. At a higher level the goals would be strategic in nature (e.g., return on sales, total cycle time), at the middle level they are tactical (e.g., delivery reliability) and there is a third operational level (e.g., capacity utilization).

Targets for KPIs

All KPIs should be accompanied by appropriate targets that will be set by management. Targets need to match up with KPIs, one to one and must be quantifiable so that the resulting performance can be benchmarked against the target. Targets should be ambitious but not over-optimistic and should be agreed with the KPI owner. They should be challenging to achieve but realistic and in line with the resources deployed by the organization for achieving them. Targets are normally set by establishing a benchmark.

The most common benchmark is historical performance. Alternatively, targets may be set based on performance levels of similar organizational units at a comparable level that facilitates benchmarking or best practices. For new KPIs with no historical reference, managers need to establish a baseline and extend out from that point forward. The following standards may also be used in setting targets:

- Absolute standards, which give the best performance that can ever be achieved. This is an ideal performance that operations might aspire to – such as the target of zero defects in total quality management.
- Competitors' standards typically through benchmarking, which looks at the performance being achieved by competitors. This is the lowest level of performance that an organization must achieve to remain competitive.

Improving and changing KPIs

KPIs are not rigid measures that are set in stone. In fact, management is entitled to consider revising, amending, withdrawing or replacing KPIs that are deemed to be irrelevant either at the outset or have become irrelevant with time and changes in strategy. As strategies and objectives develop in a dynamic environment and may change over time, it would be inappropriate to continue reporting on the same KPIs as in previous periods. Management should reflect on whether the

KPIs chosen continue to be relevant over time. Changes in KPIs and how they are measured and reported should be clearly explained.

Initiatives and action plans

For things to happen in an organization, managers must formulate and implement initiatives, and establish or initiate projects, programs and action plans. For example, improving customer service may require a new customer management system. Initiatives must be sponsored by senior management and projects should have designated owners to act as project sponsors. Initiatives are planned to include deliverables and milestones they need to have deadlines and, in most cases, funding is required. Progress towards achieving targets and milestones is always reported. Once the appropriate initiatives are launched managers must be able to meet the strategic objectives to close the loop.

Actions plans are statements of specific activities that need to be undertaken toward achieving the objective always within specific stated constraints. Action plans indicate the implementation process that will be followed towards achieving the objectives and they can be updated and modified if deemed necessary.

Bibliography

Anand, N., and Grover, N. (2015). Measuring retail supply chain performance: Theoretical model using key performance indicators (KPIs). *Benchmarking: An International Journal*, 22(1), pp. 135–166.

Badawy, M., Abd El-Aziz, A. A., Idress, A. M., Hefny, H., and Hossam, S. (2016). A survey on exploring key performance indicators. *Future Computing and Informatics Journal*, 1(1–2), pp. 47–52.

Blokdyk, G. (2022). *Metrics and KPIs*. Complete Self-Assessment Guide, UK: 5 Star Cooks.

Bressolles, G., and Lang, G. (2019). KPIs for performance measurement of e-fulfilment systems in multi-channel retailing: An exploratory study. *International Journal of Retail and Distribution Management*, 48(1), pp. 35–52.

Carlucci, D. (2010). Evaluating and selecting key performance indicators: An ANP-based model. *Measuring Business Excellence*, 14(2), pp. 66–76.

Chae, B. K. (2009). Developing key performance indicators for supply chain: An industry perspective. *Supply Chain Management: An International Journal*, 14(6), pp. 422–428.

del-Río-Ortega, A., Resinas, M., Cabanillas, C., and Ruiz-Cortés, A. (2013). On the definition and design-time analysis of process performance indicators. *Information Systems*, 38(4), pp. 470–490.

Domínguez, E., Pérez, B., Rubio, A. L., and Zapata, M. A. (2019). A taxonomy for key performance indicators management. *Computer Standards & Interfaces*, 64, pp. 24–40.

Gunasekaran, A., Patel, C., and Tirtiroglu, E. (2001). Performance measures and metrics in a supply chain environment. *International Journal of Operations & Production Management*, 21(1–2), pp. 71–87.

Hristov, I., Appolloni, A., & Chirico, A. (2022). The adoption of the key performance indicators to integrate sustainability in the business strategy: A novel five-dimensional framework. *Business Strategy and the Environment*, 31(7), pp. 3216–3230.

Marr, B. (2012). *Key Performance Indicators (KPI): The 75 Measures Every Manager Needs to Know*. Harlow: Pearson.

Parmenter, D. (2015). *Key Performance Indicators: Developing, Implementing, and Using Winning KPIs*. London: John Wiley & Sons.

Peral, J., Maté, A., and Marco, M. (2017). Application of data mining techniques to identify relevant key performance indicators. *Computer Standards & Interfaces*, 54, pp. 76–85.

Sanchez, H., and Robert, B. (2010). Measuring portfolio strategic performance using key performance indicators. *Project Management Journal*, 41(5), pp. 64–73.

Setiawan, I., and Purba, H. H. (2020). A systematic literature review of key performance indicators (KPIs) implementation. *Journal of Industrial Engineering & Management Research*, 1(3), pp. 200–208.

Wu, H. Y. (2012). Constructing a strategy map for banking institutions with key performance indicators of the balanced scorecard. *Evaluation and Program Planning*, 35(3), pp. 303–320.

CHAPTER 6

Corporate shipping KPIs

Introduction

Key performance indicators at the corporate level will be developed to reflect important corporate goals that the top management team would want to measure and monitor frequently as part of their decision-making process. Corporate level goals are those that represent the business strategy of the company and are reflected in the strategy map of the organization. Corporate KPIs reflect all the goals across the perspectives that make up the strategy of the organization. In effect, following the Balanced Scorecard notation, this means KPIs for financial goals, customer goals, internal process goals and learning and growth goals.

In the business of maritime transportation there are also several associated maritime transport goals that may be reflected in the strategy map and require the development of appropriate KPIs. Corporate level goals of maritime transport include the utilization of assets in a highly capital-intensive industry, the reduction of operating and other costs, achieving efficiency and productivity, as well as customer/marketing, operational, environmental, safety, governance and security goals.

Corporate financial key performance indicators

Financial KPIs will measure the shareholder goals of the organization. Financial KPIs will differ depending on the type of organization and its strategic financial goals. For example, a shipowning company will be more focused on the return on capital employed (ROCE) and the return on investment (ROI) compared to a third-party ship management company that will be more inclined towards measuring its revenue and market share. A shipowning company that seeks to raise funds through equity participation will be more focused on return on equity (ROE).

For most companies in the maritime industry, profitability and increase in profit will be fundamental shareholder perspective goals. Hence relevant KPIs at the corporate level should include profitability, cost and revenue KPIs. Ship owning companies or companies with a heavy asset base would also include goals and KPIs relevant to market share and return on investment. ROE will gauge the ability to invest shareholder equity contributions efficiently. Market share related KPIs would gauge the ability of the company to attract customers and increase its revenue.

A sample of possible KPIs at this level is shown in Table 6.1.

DOI: 10.4324/9781315717845-6

SHIPPING PERFORMANCE MANAGEMENT

Table 6.1 Goals and KPIs at the Financial Perspective – Corporate Level

Strategy goal	KPIs
Increase profitability	• Profit margin (net profit to net sales) • Net profit to total assets • Net income after tax • Return on net worth • Increase in number of new customers • EBITDA margins
Reduce costs	• Reduction in running costs • Reduction in OPEX • Reduction in total costs
Increase revenue	• Increase in sales • Increase in number of new customers
Investment return	• Return on capital employed (ROCE) • Return on investment (ROI) • Return in invested capital (ROIC) • Return on equity (ROE)
Market share	• Market share increase per year • Revenue increase per year • Market share increase per year • Revenue increase per year • Net sales to total sales
Cost control	• Interest expenses • Administration expenses • Cost of financing (cost of capital) • Fleet acquisition cost
OPEX	• OPEX optimization • OPEX reduction • OPEX compared to industry average
Risk	• Percentage of long-term charters • Percentage of long-term charters y-o-y • Ratio revenue time v. voyage charters • Route diversification (no of routes ships sail)
Fleet growth	• Number of vessels increase per year • Deadweight increase per year
Asset utilization	• Warehouse utilization • Ship utilization • Load factor • Crane utilization

Profitability KPIs are essential at the corporate level. Profit margin (net profit to net sales) measures net profit, after tax but before extraordinary items, expressed as a percentage of net sales. It measures the amount of net profit by each dollar of sales. Net profit to total assets measures net profit as a percentage of year-end total assets. The KPI measures return on all invested funds by both creditors and equity

54

holders. Return on net worth measures net profit as a percentage of year-end net worth (equity), i.e. it measures return on net equity invested.

Net profit to total assets seeks to measure net profit as a percentage of year-end total assets. It measures the return on all invested funds by both creditors and equity holders. Gross profit margin indicates revenues after subtracting operating expenses. A standard accounting ratio that can be used for measuring financial performance is the current ratio that measures liquidity of the company by dividing current assets by current liabilities. Current assets include cash and cash equivalents, accounts receivable, inventory, marketable securities, prepaid expenses and other liquid assets that can be readily converted to cash.

Market share position can be measured using the KPI net sales to total sales. The KPI provides an indication of what share of total available market is being captured by the company.

Cost is a major component of performance in shipping. In dry bulk shipping cost of asset acquisition and operating costs control are imperative, and relevant KPIs should be used to monitor the ability of the company to manage these costs. This includes KPIs on the cost of financing ship acquisitions (interest and cost of capital) as well as administration expenses. Operating cost control should also be gauged with relevant KPIs measuring cost reduction and cost optimization.

At the corporate level, managers would also be interested to control corporate and financing costs as well as keep an eye on cash flow. Relevant KPIs for cost control would be interest related costs, administration expenses (cost of running departments and offices) and cost of capital and fleet acquisition cost. Cost efficiency is measured by OPEX related KPIs which include cost reduction, cost optimization and benchmarking by comparison to previous periods or to an industry average.

Companies at the corporate financial level would also aim at gauging risk. There are several types of risk in the shipping industry including market risk and financial risk as well as more specific bunker price risk. In dry bulk shipping for example, market risk may be managed by considering the ratio of voyage to time charters or the routes that the company operates. Time charters are less risky as they ensure a continuous cash inflow for the company.

Corporate customer key performance indicators

Customer key performance indicators aim to align measures with business outcomes and assess things such as the value of the company to customers or the performance of the company relative to competitors.

The ability of the company to offer competitive freight rates (price related advantage) may be gauged by a set of KPIs that benchmark the company's pricing with a market average or an index such as the Baltic Dry Index. The percentage variance from the market may also be gauged. This is an important set of KPIs because it enables companies to gauge their ability to charge higher freight rates and still achieve good vessel utilization if they are able to convince the customers/

charterers of the higher technical standards of the ship or the higher levels of service quality and relationship development.

Indirect measures of competitive pricing may be reflected in the customer satisfaction index or the number of new routes opened per year. These KPIs can also be used to gauge the more generic goal of customer satisfaction. Customer satisfaction may be reflected in an overall index that may be administered to customers via a questionnaire or by developing an appropriate index using a combination of existing KPIs such as freight rates compared to market average, customer retention rate, percentage of long-term charters or other relevant KPIs that are also related to customer relationship development.

The net promoter score (NPS) is a KPI that can be used in various contexts in a set of corporate customer KPIs. The NPS is a key measure of the customers' overall perception about the company. It is calculated by asking key associates to rate the extent to which they would recommend the company. Promoters are regarded to be enthusiastic about the company, passives are those that are satisfied by vulnerable to competitive offerings and detractors those who have a negative view or experience and are likely to be negative about the organization. NPS is a leading indicator for growth and provides one of the best KPIs for gauging customer experience. The NPS can be used in conjunction with other relevant metrics, depending on the strategic goals to be measured to achieve a comprehensive and actionable view of relevant performance. Table 6.2 provides a sample of relevant KPIs for specific goals for the customer perspective at the corporate level.

Customer growth rate is measured by calculating the number of customers relative to the previous period. Marketing effectiveness can be measured using KPIs such as awareness-to-demand ratios, the cost versus leads or the cost versus sales. Such performance metrics primarily provide managers with a way to rationalize resource allocation.

Awareness level is a measure of marketing and communication effectiveness in particular. It measures the percentage of a pre-defined population that are aware of the brand of the company or the company itself or a specific campaign undertaken by the company at a given point in time. The net promoter score is also a KPI that can be used in this context.

Image held by prospects or customers is a set of measures intended to compare customers' perceptions of the firm with the perceptions they hold of other firms. Similar measures are reflected in the image held by non-customers.

Loyalty which is increasingly important in the context of shipping services, is defined as the percentage of total category spending by a customer devoted to a particular company. Companies should measure not just the longevity of relationships but also the percentage of sales from total customer spending on particular services.

Customer profitability is expressed as average dollar profit per customer or by customer group over the total lifetime relationship with the customer often expressed as a net present value. The idea is to focus attentions (such as rewards) on some key customers.

CORPORATE SHIPPING KPIS

Table 6.2 Goals and KPIs at the Customer Perspective – Corporate Level

Strategy goal	*KPIs*
Competitive freight rates	• Freight rates compared to market average • Freight rates compared to BDI/other index • Percentage of variance from market average
Customer satisfaction	• Customer satisfaction index • Freight rates compared to market average • Customer retention rate
Customer relationship	• Customer satisfaction index • Number of new routes per year • Percentage long term charters • Percentage increase in cargo coverage • Customer attrition rate • Net promoter score
Awareness level	• Percentage aware of the brand or the firm at a given point in time • Brand visibility • Net promoter score
Brand value and equity	• Brand worth • Brand visibility • Brand associations • Customer loyalty
Image held by prospects or customers	• Compare customers' perceptions of the firm with the perceptions they held of other firms (questionnaire index) • Brand value
Loyalty	• Number of years as client • Percentage share of customers' purchases • Customer retention rate
Customer profitability	• Expressed as average dollar profit per customer or by customer group over the total lifetime relationship with the customer often expressed as a net present value
Marketing effectiveness	• Cost/total spending per new customer • Promotional spending per new customer • Cost associated per lead acquisitions. • Awareness to demand ratio • Cost to leads ratio • Cost to sales ratio
Customer retention	• No of customers of > 3 years • Customer loyalty
Customer attraction	• Increase in the no of customers of < 3 years • Brand visibility
Commercial reliability	• Planned versus actual on time delivery • Damage/loss to cargo during shipment • Track and trace ability • Invoice accuracy
Customer satisfaction	• Customer satisfaction index • Days off-hire: Time asset is not available as a source of revenue

Marketing effectiveness measures reflect how well the marketing and business development function is executed at the corporate level. Relevant measures include the cost per lead acquisition which is a measure of the cost for each lead and how many leads are generated by the company's marketing efforts as well as the value of those leads.

Brand value and brand equity are key constructs in the management of any business and relevant to the customer perspective. Brand value is the monetary worth of the brand in the market. In quantitative terms it reflects the price that an investor would be prepared to pay to acquire the brand. Brand equity is a set of assets and liabilities such as brand visibility, brand associations and customer loyalty that add or subtract from the value of a current or potential product of service driven by the brand. In shipping, brand value has gained importance as companies have tried to associate brands with certain perspectives such as the environment, safety, efficiency and reliability being the main ones.

Corporate internal process key performance indicators

At the corporate level, the managers responsible to oversee internal processes will focus on certain key goals that may be relevant across the spectrum of shipping companies engaged in ship operations. Such goals include operational excellence, quality improvement and providing innovative freight solutions to customers. There is an array of KPIs that reflect internal processes within shipping companies and most of them are found at departmental or team levels (see Table 6.3). This is because most of the processes take place at lower levels in the company. Nevertheless, higher level managers are entitled to pick and choose relevant KPIs from lower levels or develop others that may reflect the internal process operations that they would like to gauge at the higher level.

Operational excellence may be reflected in a series of important measures that relate to time wasted or missed deadlines (off-hire, missed laycan) or an overall voyage planning efficiency index. The voyage planning efficiency may be developed as an aggregate index of KPIs such as number of missed laycan, number of days delay, off-hires, and vessel scheduling to be gauged by number of delays, and on time delivery rate.

One of the most significant voyage costs is the cost of bunker fuel. Hence, managers at the higher levels of the hierarchy may want to track the ability of internal processes to procure fuel efficiently and at competitive prices. Such measures include bunker procurement efficiency (hours delay), bunker DIFOT and average years of bunker supplier relationships.

Maintaining quality standards may be measured by KPIs that include the ability to obtain and maintain quality certifications such as ISO standards, having an environmental performance index, a safety performance index and a risk management index. At corporate level, managers would prefer an overall index for performance rather than be engaged in micro-managing aspects that are relevant to the departments of even fleet or team levels. On this basis, it is recommended to develop relevant indices that reflect environmental, safety or risk management performance (e.g. number of incident investigation and analysis, number of observations etc.).

Table 6.3 Goals and KPIs at the Internal Process Perspective – Corporate Level

Strategy goal	KPIs
Operational excellence	• Number of off-hire days • Average years of supplier relationships • Voyage planning efficiency index • Bunker cost variance from industry average • Bunker DIFOT
Safety	• Safety index • ISM conformance index
Quality	• ISO certification • Environmental index • Safety index
Innovative freight solutions	• Number of new long-term contracts • Increase in spot fixtures • Number of new supply chains served • Asset utilization • Chartering effectiveness index
Environmental performance	• Percentage of eco-friendly standard ships • Percentage of fuel-efficient ships • Average fleet age
Cost control performance	• Total cost deviation from budget • OPEX percentage change to market • OPEX percentage change to previous quarter • OPEX percentage deviation from budget

Another two areas for monitoring in the context of internal processes include environmental performance and cost control performance. Companies should have in place processes for ensuring compliance to environmental performance standards as indicated by the organization's environmental policy. At the same time processes to monitor and control major cost elements of the company's operation should be in place and appropriate KPIs should be developed. The KPIs relate to fuel efficiency, eco-friendly vessels; and the fleet age which is a proxy for more environmentally friendly vessels. The major cost element is the operating costs of ships (OPEX) hence relevant KPIs may monitor change in OPEX compared to market average or to other internally set standards such as the budget.

Table 6.3 provides a sample of relevant KPIs.

Corporate learning and growth key performance indicators

At corporate level the main KPIs at the learning and growth perspective will be related to the ability of improving human capital, management effectiveness, corporate governance and adoption of technology.

At corporate level, the KPIs should be of an aggregate nature and reflect overall performance. Hence, at this level it is advisable to use indices instead of disaggregated measures that will be monitored at lower (e.g. department) level. Key indices that can be used to reflect and monitor performance include the staff satisfaction index, the safety culture index and the cost culture index. Companies may also want to develop an index of corporate governance which will be made up of relevant corporate governance KPIs such as 'Presence of independent internal auditor (auditing)', 'Number of meetings of audit committee (auditing)', and 'Number of observations of non-compliance to financial transparency and information disclosure'. In addition, other KPIs for corporate governance may be used as shown in Table 6.4. Technological capital may be monitored through the investment made in new technology and innovation.

Table 6.4 provides a sample of relevant KPIs.

Table 6.4 Goals and KPIs at the Learning and Growth Perspective – Corporate Level

Strategy goal	*KPIs*
Training	• Training hours per employee per period • Dollars invested in training per employee per year • Total amount of dollars invested in human resource training
Personnel turnover	• Total employee turnover rate • Senior employee retention rate
Staff satisfaction	• Staff satisfaction index • Employee retention rate
Improve human capital	• Competency profile (qualifications/training/no of years' experience) • Employee retention rate • Talent acquisition rate • Employee performance • Safety culture index • Cost culture index
Management effectiveness	• Number of years in senior positions (management industry expertise) • Management effectiveness (questionnaire index) • Knowledge management (questionnaire index)
Corporate governance	• Corporate governance index • Presence of independent internal auditor (auditing) • Number of meetings of audit committee (auditing) • Number of independent directors (Board and management structure and process) • Number of BoD meetings without management presence • Number of corporate responsibility initiatives • Number of instances of financial reporting in non-compliance to international standards • Number of observations of non-compliance to financial transparency and information disclosure • Shareholders with additional voting rights (ownership structure and exercise of control right)
Technological capital	• Dollars invested in IT • Dollars invested in ship related technology • Dollars in ship/system upgrades

Bibliography

Bauer, K. (2004). KPIs – The metrics that drive performance management. *DM Review*, 14(9), p. 63.

Domínguez, E., Pérez, B., Rubio, A. L., and Zapata, M. A. (2019). A taxonomy for key performance indicators management. *Computer Standards & Interfaces*, 64, pp. 24–40.

Figge, F., Hahn, T., Schaltegger, S., and Wagner, M. (2002). The sustainability balanced scorecard – Linking sustainability management to business strategy. *Business Strategy and the Environment*, 11(5), pp. 269–284.

Kerzner, H. (2013). *Project Management Metrics, KPI, and Dashbords: A Guide to Measuring and Monitoring Project Performance*. Hoboken, New Jersey: John Wiley and Sons, Inc.

Maiga, A., and Jacobs, F. (2003). Balanced scorecard, activity-based costing and company performance: An empirical analysis. *Journal of Managerial Issues*, 15(3), pp. 283–301.

Marr, B. (2011). Key performance indicators: The 75 measures every manager needs to know. *Financial Times*.

Parmenter, D. (2015). *Key Performance Indicators: Developing, Implementing, and Using Winning KPIs*. Hoboken, New Jersey: John Wiley & Sons.

Smith, S., and Heijden, H. (2017). Analysts' evaluation of KPI usefulness, standardization and assurance. *Journal of Applied Accounting Research*, 18(1), pp. 63–86.

CHAPTER 7

Case studies of maritime and shipping companies

Introduction

The cases in this chapter aim to simulate the strategy of chosen companies from data that are available in the public domain. Conceptualization is used for the study of the strategies and the possible choice of key performance indicators. Companies in the public domain are subject to scrutiny and application of theoretical models and this is what this chapter illustrates, the study of real-life companies through published data and the conceptualization of their strategy and KPIs. The studies herein do not necessarily depict the actual intended strategies or evaluate the merits or otherwise of any company strategy, but rather illustrate the strategies as published and develop possible KPIs to measure strategic goals. In addition, the companies are not identified by name and characteristics have been altered so that anonymity is fully preserved.

Company A: A dry bulk shipping company

Description

The company was formed initially to meet rising demand for shipping cargo into and out of India. The company has a fleet of diversified bulk carriers of medium and large size including Supramax, Capesize and Panamax vessels. The vessels are Japanese built and are designed for high-performance and environmentally friendly operations. The company may also charter vessels from the market or from associated companies that boast large dry bulk fleets.

Vision and mission

The objectives are reflected in the company's vision and mission statements. The vision of the company indicates that the company aims to become a leading bulk carrier in the Indian market but also globally and serve the needs of its main customer which is a parent company.

The company has developed business strategy, policies and values that focus on the development of a world class fleet, excellence in operation, and aim to offer

62   DOI: 10.4324/9781315717845-7

to their clients, innovative freight solutions and increasing value to all stakeholders whilst remaining committed to the highest standards of safety, environmental performance and corporate governance.

The company is committed to developing a very effective and efficient workforce and sustainable internal processes that would create and deliver customer as well as stakeholder value, through innovation, excellence and integrity.

Strategy goals

The company has a quality management system in place to ensure safety and adherence to strict standards of operation that are regularly reviewed and updated. It also adopted business practices that contribute towards sustainability and aim to minimize the carbon footprint by reducing greenhouse gas emissions and by adopting relevant technological advances to minimize pollution to the marine environment.

The company delivers a different type of value to its customers that includes competitive freight rates, safe and reliable transportation, timely delivery of cargo and accurate post fixture documentation, innovative freight solutions and long-term freight structuring. These goals are achieved by having the appropriate processes and people.

The objectives of the company in serving its clients can be used to develop its value proposition. The company defined its customers as the parent group and others outside the group and has developed two broad geographical segments viz. the Indian market and other global customers.

In terms of offerings, the company can provide eco-friendly vessels that would primarily operate in the Asia Pacific and Atlantic regions but would also engage in cross trade between Atlantic and Pacific trades. The company is able to operate worldwide in a multitude of trade routes, carrying a wide range of cargoes to fulfil the needs of its varied customer base.

Customers are conferred specific advantages and value. For instance, the company offers diversity in carriage capacities and flexibility to serve different customer segments across a wide spectrum of businesses and geographies. It also offers long term voyage and time charters through innovative freight structures, which help customers gain control of their costs and manage their supply chain effectively.

Very important hallmarks of what the company offers are the competitive freight rates, diverse routes and a diverse fleet mix, operational excellence, customer focus, speed, flexibility and innovative freight solutions.

In terms of its business processes and how the company delivers value to its customers, the company has attained ISO 9001: 2008 and ISO 14001: 2004 certifications which reinforces the long-term goal of having strong processes with high quality and environmental standards. The company applies best practices in operational processes, has a highly competent team of motivated employees and places emphasis on innovation, ethics, integrity and corporate governance.

Strategy and KPIs

Company A aims to be a leading player in the dry bulk segment on a global scale. Consistent with its vision statement, the company has a large and varied fleet of ships which was developed together with high quality service capability in order to meet the demand for dry bulk materials. The company strives to establish a reputation in the international shipping industry for operating and maintaining a fleet with high standards of performance, reliability and safety. Backed by a highly competent, motivated team with strong shipping expertise, the company aspires to create consistent value for its customers and stakeholders. The company believes that building strategic partnerships through customized freight solutions will be the key driver in its relationship with its customers.

The company exhibits strong strategic performance in terms of its social corporate responsibility as it is committed to meet the highest level of compliance to environment and safety regulations, spanning onshore and on-board operations.

The strategy map is developed around the four perspectives of the Balanced Scorecard. In the shareholder perspective the ultimate goal is to increase shareholder value by achieving increase in revenue, profitability, fleet growth and control of expenses and the cost structure. It is also in the interests of shareholders to manage risk in the context of being a dry bulk shipping company.

In terms of the customer perspective the company has defined its key goals at corporate level as the fulfilment and satisfaction of its customers. In this context the company has two types of customers, viz., the parent company and external third-party customers. The key strategic goals are fulfilment of the cargo requirements of the group and fulfilment of the requirements of customers in the global markets where the company is currently operating. In addition, the company aims to develop a close customer relationship with both internal and external customers and this is reflected in both its vision and mission statements.

In terms of its internal processes the company's goals make particular reference to its operations processes particularly with respect to sustainability and the environment. One of the key challenges faced in dry bulk shipping logistics is the impact on the environment particularly with regard to the emissions of dry bulk carriers. Companies need to comply with air and water pollution legislation. For example, since 2020, IMO rules prohibit ships from using fuels with a sulfur content above 0.5%, compared with the previous level of 3.5%, unless they are equipped with so-called scrubbers to clean up sulfur emissions. This is enforced by fines levied by the IMO's member states. The company also needs to comply with IMOs Carbon Intensity Indicator (CII) which monitors emission of carbon dioxide of ships per cargo-carrying capacity and nautical mile. The objective is to reduce the environmental carbon footprint of vessels by restricting emissions and improving fuel consumption. Vessels should not achieve a rating below D, otherwise they must submit and implement an improvement plan.

It is also important for the company to have the processes required to deliver innovative freight solutions to the clients. Such processes will be operationalized when customers' requirements deviate from the norm and there is a need to respond quickly to cater for new cargoes, new ports, new supply chains or a new type of ship that may be required by the customer. The process must be in place for the company to deliver a freight solution that responds to the new customer requirement. Operating costs must be controlled, and processes must be in place monitoring this. Such processes may be established at department level since they relate to department tasks such as purchasing related processes, crew recruitment and crew management processes and other operational processes. For these processes, departments will need to develop relevant objectives and targets at that level.

Other goals in the internal process perspective include for example, to ensure that the organization operates in accordance to the procedures and standards of quality systems (e.g. ISO).

In terms of organizational learning and growth the company's strategy refers to three specific themes including human capital, information capital and corporate governance. Hence the company must ensure efficient recruitment, retention and development of employees, investment in technology to facilitate efficient information exchange and adoption of corporate governance principles that would safeguard the interests of shareholders.

The main elements of the company's vision statement reflect the goals 'to be a leading bulk carrier company' which can be measured by KPIs such as sales, market share, revenue growth and profitability among others. At the same time the company aims to be 'a strategic partner for its parent group', 'operating on a global scale' with 'credible and sustainable ship operations' offering 'high quality innovative freight solutions' and 'upholding the highest standards in terms of safety, environmental protection and corporate governance'. The latter is a clear indication of the existence of an ESG policy for this organization.

Based on the identified goals Table 7.1 illustrates possible KPIs for this dry bulk shipping company.

Company B: A liner shipping company

Description

Company B is one of the world's biggest liner container shipping companies, operating more than 15% of the world's container fleet and transporting about 3% of the world's global seaborne trade. The ships of the company make more than 75,000 port calls per year servicing more than 100,000 customers. The company has a very large and young fleet of owned and chartered container vessels of more than 4 million TEU and operates on a strategy whereby it charters about 50% of its fleet from other third-party owners; a strategy that is adopted almost universally in liner shipping.

Table 7.1 Dry Bulk Shipping Company KPIs – Corporate Level

Perspective	Strategic goal	KPIs
Shareholder value	Revenue	Sales
		Market share
		Increase in revenue per year
	Expenses	Interest expenses
		Administration expenses
		Cost of financing
		Fleet acquisition cost
	Profit	Profit after tax
		ROIC
		ROE
	Risk	Percentage long term charters
		Route diversification
	Fleet growth	Number of vessels increase per year
		Total fleet compared to previous period
		Total DWT compared to previous period
Customer value	Customer relationship	Customer satisfaction index
		Competitive freight rates (percentage variance from market)
		Number of new routes per year
	Group cargo coverage	Percentage cargo coverage
		Total tonnes carried per period
	Global markets	Percentage increase cargo coverage
		Number of new customers
		Percentage customer retention
Internal processes	Operational excellence	Bunker procurement efficiency/DIFOT
		Average years supplier relationships
		Voyage planning (number of missed laycan, number of days delay, bunker cost variance from industry average), Vessel scheduling (number of delays, on time delivery rate, number of missed laycan)
		Chartering efficiencies (on-time delivery, off-hires)
	Sustainable operations	Carbon Intensity Indicator Index (CII)
		Energy Efficiency Design Index (EEDI)
		Energy Efficiency Operational Indicator (EEOI)
	Innovative freight solutions	Number of new long-term contracts
		Increase in spot fixtures
		Number of new supply chains served
		Asset utilization (speed of chartering-in)
	Improve quality	ISO certifications
		Improving environment and safety indices
		Risk management (number of incident investigation and analysis, number of observations)

Perspective	Strategic goal	KPIs
	World fleet class profile	Percentage of ships chartered-in Type/size of vessels (mix) Percentage of eco-friendly ships Percentage of fuel-efficient ships
	Operating costs	Percentage change in OPEX versus market Percentage deviation from budget OPEX compared to previous quarter OPEX compared to last year
Learning and growth	Information capital	Industry expertise (years in market) Management effectiveness (questionnaire index) Knowledge management (questionnaire index) Dollars invested in IT
	Corporate governance	G-index of corporate governance Auditing (independence of internal auditor/audit committee) Board and management structure and process (independent directors, BoD meetings without management presence) Financial reporting in compliance to international standards Financial transparency and information disclosure Ownership structure and exercise of control right
	Human capital	Competency profile (qualifications/training/ number of years' experience) Employee retention rate Talent acquisition rate Performance measurement (employee performance) Culture (safety culture index, cost culture index)

Vision and mission

The vision of the company is to be an integrated container logistics company working to connect and simplify its customers' supply chain while the mission is to enable and facilitate global supply chains and provide opportunities for its customers to trade globally.

Strategy and KPIs

In terms of strategy the company has a large part of its business (approximately 50%) tied up in long-term contracts (e.g., one year duration), also selling short term contracts of about one month duration. The company has a group of major clients (25%) and another 15% of business agreed with freight forwarders.

Company B offers an extensive service range, connecting hundreds of ports globally, achieving this through a network of own routes and in collaboration with others in the form of strategic alliances. Company B can transport any type of specialized or sensitive cargo. Company B also offers added value services, such as door-to-door transportation and logistics services. To achieve this, the company has an extensive inland intermodal network and feeder connections to smaller ports not serviced by larger container vessels. As mentioned, the company also boasts a comparably young fleet (in terms of ships' average age).

The company aims to offer to its customers a reliable service, evidenced by its performance on goals such as on-time delivery and integrated scheduling of shipments. Reliability is an important advantage for product supply chains as it provides the opportunity to reach the target markets on time and avoid costs of inventory. The company works with port terminals to reduce port time and thus contribute to the supply chain goals of its customers.

Another customer-oriented goal of Company B is to simplify the shipping process for its customers. The shipping process consists of the transportation flow as well as the information flow that is associated with the goods. The information flow is facilitated through digitalization allowing customers to have access to relevant information and complements the very efficient process of physical transportation.

In addition to the previous points, the company has long considered that one of the key criteria for container transportation purchasing by customers would be the environmental performance of the liner company. In this context, the company sought to become a leader in low carbon footprint performance by reducing carbon dioxide emissions and minimizing the impact of its operations on the marine environment. It was also among the first companies to order ships that were environmentally friendly and is committed and fully engaged in responsible ship recycling through the principle of ship cradle-to-cradle passport. In this context the company also adopted the principles of slow-steaming in order to improve environmental conservation and at the same time reduce costs associated with fuel consumption. Slow steaming is facilitated by having bigger ships and thus carrying more cargo and achieving scale economies. Another performance-related principle adopted by the company is the use of ship performance data to make incremental improvements to consumptions particularly by adjusting speeds and routes based on weather, currents and port delays. Data are collected using advanced information technology from Automatic Identification System (AIS) and on-board sensors.

The company targets large shippers, freight forwarders and other leading international customers on a geographical segmentation basis (Asia Pacific, Europe, Americas, Middle East and Africa). Based on the previous explanation, what is depicted in Table 7.2 could reflect the goals and key performance indicators of the liner shipping company at corporate level.

CASE STUDIES OF MARITIME AND SHIPPING COMPANIES

Table 7.2 Liner Shipping Company KPIs – Corporate Level

Perspective	Strategic goal	KPIs
Shareholder value	Growth	Number of new ships delivered per time-period
		Percentage market share relative to competitors
		Increase in volumes per key customer
		Number of vessels increase/year
		Percentage share of onshore transport by railway line or river line
	Profit	Percentage of net income growth
		Percentage of average revenue growth per TEU
		EBITDA margins
	Cost reduction	Administration expenses
		Percentage of actual vs budgeted cost difference
		Cost of fleet acquisition
	Capacity utilization	Percentage of fleet capacity utilization per TEU
		Load factor
Customer value	Reliability	Port-to-port transit time against schedule
		Delay/on-time shipment of cargo
		Customer Satisfaction Index
		Speed of chartering-in
		Elapsed time between shipping instruction and bill of lading issue
		Percentage asset utilization over the supply chain
	Schedule reliability	Port-to-port transit time against schedule
		Time delay in ship arrivals
		Time delay in ship departure
	Transit time	Port-to-port transit time against schedule
		Delay/on-time shipment of cargo
		Elapsed time between shipping instruction and bill of lading issue
	Frequency	Frequency rate
		Number of sailings per route per time period
	Route network	Number of new routes per year
		Percentage of new to total routes
		Number of new customers
		Number of new supply chains served
	Value added services	Number of new supply chain services
		Revenue from new services (developed in the last year)
		Competitive freight rates (percentage variance from market)

(Continued)

Table 7.2 (Continued)

Perspective	Strategic goal	KPIs
	Customer service	Percentage customer retention
		Number of customized or end to end service compared with number of all service
		Customer Satisfaction Index
		Number of complaints received per order
		Number of new long-term contracts
		Customer give-up rate/discontinue a service
		Growth of cargo shipment per customer
Internal processes	Safety	Number of fatal accidents
		Number of containers lost
		Number of permanent/partial disabilities
		Number of lost working hours per year
		Lost-time injury frequency
	Operational efficiency	Percentage of certified operational processes
		Days/number of delays and on time delivery rate
		Planned vs actual chartering efficiencies (on-time delivery/shipment of cargo)
		Port dwell times
		Inland transit time
		Number of TEUs transported intermodally
		Number of operational related deficiencies
		Order process cycle time (days)
Learning and growth	HR capability	Employee satisfaction index (survey)
		Career management and diversity (rate of men to women at managerial positions)
		Index of quality of life and well-being at work
		Training hours of employee per year
		Number of employees attended classroom & e-learning courses
		Training budget per period
	Sustainability	Percentage investment share on sustainability
		Number of developed eco-solutions
		Non-compliance incidents with major international regulation
		Energy Efficiency Design Index (EEDI)

Perspective	Strategic goal	KPIs
	Transformation	Integration of system (e-business) with customer, agent, and partners (data exchange frequency, order processing speed)
		No of eco-technologies usage per year
		No of smart service/one stop services per year
		Digital service efficiency compared with competitor (process efficiency, system fail, data security, accuracy of invoices, accuracy of traceability)
	ESG	Carbon Intensity Index (CII)
		Energy Efficiency Existing Ship Index (EEXI)
		Environmental index performance
		Percentage investment share on sustainability
		Invested dollars on alternative fuels
		Rate of return on digital technology investment
		Number of new eco-solutions adopted
		Number of non-compliance incidents with major international regulations
		Number of social related contributions
		Career management and diversity (rate of men to women at managerial positions)
		Corporate governance index performance

Company C: A tanker company

Description

Company C is one of the largest tanker companies in the world operating ships and moving cargoes in the global energy supply chain. Its mission has been defined as facilitating the global energy supply chain by providing a vital link between producers and consumers. Since its inception it grew from a tanker operator to a leader in the marine midstream energy supply chain.

Vision and mission

The company's vision refers to its role in serving the global energy supply chain including oil and gas and its mission states that the company aims to be the first choice of customers in the shipping industry, to uphold quality and built brand value and at the same time to create value for its shareholders.

Strategy and KPIs

The strategy of the company has been to achieve growth through the management of assets such as tanker, shuttle tankers, product tankers, FPSOs, FSOs, LNG, LPG and specialized floating regasification and liquefaction plants. The company aims to achieve a competitive advantage by offering a diversified product portfolio to its clients including a comprehensive set of marine services. It does so through the development of a huge portfolio of assets (more than 160 owned ships), specialized and competent human resources (about 5,500 employees), and the development of client and partner relationships.

The company aims to offer customer solutions by providing a wide range of vessel types and expensive service range as a global operator linking production and consumption markets. It also operates in specialized higher value-added segments such as LNG, LPG and CNG. It aims to achieve operational excellence with a sustainability-oriented direction. The company aims at providing customer added value services including logistics related services. The scope is to be able to offer to the customer everything under one roof and thus achieve a high level of cross-sales. Development of customer relationships and customer commitment and retention are essential parts of the strategy. The company manages risk by operating in spot and time charter markets.

The company deploys certain resources and has developed specific capabilities and human skills to achieve value creation for customers and stakeholders. The company has nurtured the development of strong technical and operational skills and encourages the adoption of innovation be it in project management, in quality and safe tanker operations and in environmental practices which includes the sustainability and emissions control programme.

Based on the aforementioned strategic goals, possible KPIs for this tanker shipping company are as shown in Table 7.3.

Table 7.3 Tanker Shipping Company KPIs – Corporate Level

Perspective	Strategic goal	KPIs
Shareholder value	Profitability	Profit margin
		EBTDA
	Revenue	Sales
		Market share
		Increase in revenue per year
	Cost reduction	Percentage of actual vs budgeted cost difference
		Cost of fleet acquisition
		OPEX compared to market average
Customer value	Extensive service range	Number of energy supply chains served
		Number of customers
		Increase in number of customers over previous period
		Ship type diversification index

CASE STUDIES OF MARITIME AND SHIPPING COMPANIES

Perspective	Strategic goal	KPIs
	Customer value added logistics	Number of new long-term contracts
		Percentage customer retention
		Number of customized or end to end service compared with number of all services
		Revenue from new services (developed in the last year)
	Customer relations	Number of new long-term contracts
		Customer Satisfaction Index
		Customer retention rate
Internal processes	Innovation	Number of new process updates per time period
		Number of new supply chains served
		Revenue from new services
	Centralized quality	Number of quality certificates
		Number of quality awards
		Number of incidents
		Safety index
		TMSA Index
	Risk management	Percentage of long-term charters
		Safety index
		Spot v time charter contracts
	Operational excellence	Number of off-hires
		Investment in planned repair and maintenance
		Spending in repairs
	Emissions control programme	CO_2 efficiency (emitted mass of CO_2 to the ship's total transport work)
		NOx efficiency (NOx emitted relative to the transport work performed)
		SOx efficiency (emitted mass of SOx emitted relative to the transport work performed)
		Carbon Intensity Index (CII)
		Energy Efficiency Existing Ship Index (EEXI)
Learning and growth	Staff loyalty	Employee Satisfaction Index
		Employee Retention Rate
	Strong technical skills	Hours of training per employee per hour
		Percentage of acceptable training scores
		Number of trainings attended for new systems

Company D: Containership charter owner

Description

The company used to be a traditional general cargo ship owning company that operated multi-purpose vessels. Following a family succession, the company implemented a strategy that focused on the acquisition of large modern containerships which would then be chartered out to international liner shipping companies. Before the transition the fleet consisted of three bulk carriers. In the early 1990s, the company began to dramatically expand its fleet, beginning with the acquisition of 2,700 TEU containerships, which were subsequently chartered out on long-term charters. The company's growth was spectacular between 1993 to 2005 with its containership capacity expanding at a 32% annual compound rate.

The growth of the company occurred organically though multiple shipping cycles and was aided by key strategic goals such as the development of customer relationships, focusing on impeccable service quality and the exploitation of market opportunities by understanding the cyclicality of market and demand and supply workings. After cementing its positioning in the market, the company also went public in the New York Stock Exchange (NYSE). Its fleet has reached more than 65 owned containerships. In addition to organic growth, the company also engaged in acquisitions.

Vision and mission

The vision of the company reflects its commitment to be the preferred supplier of containerships to its customers who are mainly leading liner shipping companies and to enable them to offer integrated logistics solutions. The future aspiration of the company is to offer quality ships and premium services to its customer base, to expand their fleet and connect ships and crew innovatively. According to its mission statement, Company D aims to achieve the aforementioned vision by utilizing its solid operational, technical and financial resources and by continuing to provide outstanding customer service, enforce rigorous operational standards, maintain a steadfast commitment to safety and environmental protection and reward its shareholders.

Strategy and KPIs

The company aims to capitalize on growth opportunities in the container shipping industry and has set the following strategic goals:

- Grow the business
- Increase earnings
- Maximize value for shareholders
- Provide a high level of customer service

- Diversify its charter portfolio (long and short-term charters)
- Be selective in second-hand and newbuilding vessel acquisitions
- Invest in larger containerships

The company's strategy is centred around serving the needs of its customers with a high standard of service quality by focusing on the safety of the crews, the operational excellence of its vessels and the pursuit of technological innovation. The company purports to apply a focused business model that facilitated survival through troughs and prosperity through the highs of multiple economic cycles. The company seems to be well-positioned to participate in each growth cycle and continue to be an industry consolidator.

The company considers its sources of competitive advantage to include:

- The average age of its containership fleet which is low coupled with a reputation for safety and quality
- The reputation of the company for operational excellence and technological leadership
- Long-standing relationships with leading liner companies (10 out of the top 20 are current customers)
- Cash flow stability through multi-year charters (5–8 years)
- Strong financial results and flexibility

The value proposition of the company addresses the three key questions of the target customers segment(s) (addressing the who question), what is the product offering that creates customer value (addressing the what question) and how the company will create and deliver value to customers and shareholders. The customers are principally segmented into two major groups. The first group includes all leading container lines (e.g., Maersk, Cosco etc.) and the second group are all other companies operating in all geographic regions.

Value is created by offering to the customer the following benefits:

- Large containerships
- Strong relationships
- Reputation
- Operational excellence
- Technological excellence
- High quality and cost efficiency
- IT services for the customer value chain

The company has developed capabilities to enable it to put into productive use its assets and resources and as a result to create value. Key resources and capabilities include:

- Strong IT and logistics capabilities
- Low average fleet age
- Mixture of old and new assets

- Innovation in operations and technological applications
- Chartering in/out and sale and purchase effectiveness

The company has established a strong reputation for technological leadership and is widely regarded as an innovator in the industry and has developed many design and software solutions that have benefited its clients. The company takes pride in the pioneering role it has played in developing technological platforms that serve its clients and other industry stakeholders and participants. The company is focused on the creation of customer value. One key criterion for customer value is advanced operational capability and ship reliability. To achieve its operational goals, the company consults with its customers, charterers, leading shipyards and classification societies in order to design and built ships that would achieve speed, engine and cargo handling efficiencies through the application of advanced technology. Reliability is achieved through the investment in maintenance and inspection programmes using the latest technological advances.

The key goals of the company include:

- Pro-active application of international standards and regulations
- Quality service
- Innovation in energy efficiency improvements
- Being a preferred carrier for charterers
- Developing a reputation for excellence in container shipping and in customer service
- Safety and quality ashore and on-board
- Strict adherence to environmental laws and regulations

The company has placed emphasis on research and development aimed at developing advanced tools to monitor and optimize fuel efficiency, emissions control, energy management and bunkers control. In addition to the initiatives described previously, the implementation of an online data acquisition and processing platform to provide accurate and real-time control of vessels' operational parameters maintains a technological edge. Among the objectives of the company is to be an innovator in operational and technological aspects of container shipping and this includes the development of appropriate software and technological capabilities for container and logistics transportation. The company operates under high quality standards and has achieved certification from recognized classification societies. The company and its affiliates have invested in the areas of crew recruitment and crew training. Crew recruitment is facilitated by a hands-on approach in the selection and control of seafarer employment through owned crewing offices. This ensures the recruitment of experienced and qualified crew. They are also providing enhanced training to their seafarers facilitating reliability in servicing their vessels.

Based on the strategic goals of the company the following KPIs may be developed as illustrated in Table 7.4.

Table 7.4 Container Charter Owner Shipping Company KPIs – Corporate Level

Perspective	Strategic goal	KPIs
Shareholder value	Large containerships	Relative increase in number of ships per period
		Relative increase in TEU capacity per period
	Sustainability of earnings	Revenue year-on-year
		Sales growth rate
	Profit	Percentage of net income growth
		Percentage of average revenue growth per TEU
		EBITDA Margins
	Ship financing	Cost of financing
		Fleet acquisition cost
	Fleet mix decisions	Rate of new buildings to second-hand acquisitions per year
Customer value	Customer relationship	Customer retention rate
		Number of long-term charters
	Operational excellence	Percentage change in OPEX versus market
		Percentage deviation from budget
		OPEX compared to previous quarter
		OPEX compared to last year
	Quality service	Number of new customers
		Quality certifications
		Customer satisfaction
		Customer retention rate
Internal processes	Operational excellence	Number of off-hires
		Number of detentions
	High quality	Low average fleet age
		Mixture of old and new assets
		Chartering in/out and S&P effectiveness
	Safety	Safety index (LTIF, cargo incidents, navigational incidents, PSC detention, number of injuries, number of spills to environment, accidents, near misses, detentions, non-conformities)
		Percentage change in safety observations from external audits
		Lost time incident (crew)
		Average time to respond to an urgent incident
	Energy efficiency	Dollars invested in energy efficiency improvements
		Energy Efficiency Existing Ship Index (EEXI)

(*Continued*)

Table 7.4 (Continued)

Perspective	Strategic goal	KPIs
	Quality and international standards	Number of MARPOL violations
		Safety index
		Percentage change in safety observations from audits
	Environment	Number of MARPOL violations
		Gas emission records
		Energy Efficiency Existing Ship Index (EEXI)
		Carbon Intensity Index (CII)
	Technical effectiveness	Compliance to class rules
		Port state detention based on technical issues
		Number of critical equipment failure
	Crewing effectiveness	Average time to crew a vessel
		Number of seafarers employed
		Average number of cadets on board
	Innovation in operations and technological applications	Number of new IT innovations per year
		Dollars investment in new technology
Learning and growth	Strong IT and logistics	Number of new logistics innovations per year
		Revenue from new logistics services
	Innovation	Revenue from new IT services
		Number of new IT innovations per year
	Technical skills	Hours of training per employee per hour
		Percentage of acceptable training scores
		No of training for new systems

Company E: Third-party ship management

Description

Third-party ship management entails the organization of operational and economic activities for the ship on behalf of its owner to ensure that it is a sustainable revenue earning entity. Third-party ship management involves the management of ships on behalf of owners and ship management services include crewing and technical management (full management) as well as the provision of other incidental and ancillary services such as commercial management.

The core values of the company are centred around having a long-term focus on third party ship management and adopting an entrepreneurial approach, coupled with rigorous risk management, service orientation and reliability. The company prides itself for the respect towards its employees by providing them with opportunities for continuous development and learning and treating them fairly. In addition, the focus on the business partners and adhering to the highest ethical standards nurtures the outstanding reputation of the company.

Strategy and KPIs

Relevant strategic goals of the company include the ability to develop and maintain the company's reputation particularly on issues that are important for the customer such as cost efficiency, operational excellence and provision of service solutions.

At the shareholder level, important goals for ship management include profitability, cash-flow, fleet growth and maintaining brand value. As a business that comparably does not require high capital investments, shareholders would be naturally more focused on revenues, cost and cash flows. Revenues are reflected in the number of customers and the number of ships under management. Relevant goals for profit, cash flow, cost performance, brand and fleet growth require accurate key performance indicators a sample of which are shown in Table 7.5. The KPIs will be used to measure goals of the ship management company at corporate level.

Customers of ship management companies will be interested in keeping track of such goals as vessel cost-efficiency (the ship's operating costs), the ship's earning period (minimize off-hires), asset preservation, price reliability, operational reliability and service range, whereas the company would also want to gauge customer satisfaction.

Internal process goals measure the ability of accomplishing important ship management tasks internally by following pre-determined courses of action that may be stated in manuals at lower levels. Important internal processes for ship management include crewing, maintenance of safety standards, purchasing effectiveness, technical and innovation effectiveness. KPIs for internal processes to achieve the goals are shown in Table 7.5.

The learning and growth perspective at corporate level invariably focuses on the achievement of goals that relate to improvement in the value of resources, knowledge and technology within the organization. The relevant KPIs are shown in Table 7.5.

SHIPPING PERFORMANCE MANAGEMENT

Table 7.5 Ship Management Company KPIs – Corporate Level

Perspective	Strategic goal	KPIs
Shareholder value	Profitability	Profit margin
		Net income after tax
		Running costs
		Retention of existing customers
		Cross-sales increase
	Cost performance	Percentage change in company costs per vessel
		Operating cost optimization
	Revenue growth	Cross-sales increase
		Increase in revenue
		Increase in new customers
	Cash flow	Bad debt
		Working capital
	Brand	External recognition index
		Number of international presentations per year
		Number of tier-1 clients attracted
	Fleet growth	Number of vessels increase per year
		Number of new customers per year
		Retention rate of customers
Customer value	Earning period	Number of off-hire days
		Revenue change per period
		Earning period in days
	Cost	OPEX compared to industry average
		OPEX compared to previous period
		Percentage deviation from budget
		Average running costs per day per ship type and age
	Asset preservation	Years of service
		Planned maintenance observations
	Operational reliability	Off-hire days
		Fleet availability measure (Actual fleet availability – planned availability)/total available days
		Port State Control detentions
		Number of MARPOL violations
	Satisfaction	Retention of existing customers
		Number of formal communication (personalized service)
		Number of service customization

80

Perspective	Strategic goal	KPIs
	Client relationships	Average number of years a client is retained
		Percentage change in number of formal client complaints
	Price reliability	Vessel budget variance
		Percentage deviation from budget (OPEX, other budgets)
		Average running costs per day per ship type and age
	Service range	Increase in services
		Number of services offered
Internal processes	Purchasing effectiveness	Quotes received per purchase
		Cost of supplies (yearly benchmark)
		Deviation from budget
	Safety and environment	Safety index (LTIF, cargo incidents, navigational incidents, PSC detention, number of injuries, number of spills to environment, accidents, near misses, detentions, non-conformities)
		Percentage change in safety observations from external audits
		Lost time incident (crew)
		Number of MARPOL violations
		Average time to respond to an urgent incident
	Crewing effectiveness	Speed of access
		Optimal cost
		Number of seafarers retained
		Number of early terminations
		Percentage of crew relieved on time
	Technical effectiveness	Compliance to class rules
		Port state detention based on technical issues
		Number of critical equipment failure
	Innovation effectiveness	Number of new services in the last year
		Time to market new services
Learning and growth	Human value	Training budget
		Number of training sessions per year per person
		Retention rate of officers
		Retention rate of seafarers
		Retention rate of shore staff
		Personnel certification (competency)
		Performance pay level (bonus percentage achieved)
		Number of seafarers in database

(*Continued*)

Table 7.5 (Continued)

Perspective	Strategic goal	KPIs
	Business knowledge	Number of training for new systems
		Number of communication equipment upgrades
		Number of other equipment upgrades
	Effective leadership	Significant positive change in management effectiveness index
		Number of audit findings outstanding six months later
		Number of best practices implemented
		Percentage of departments achieving performance bonus
	Safety culture	Number of violations from internal audits
		Number of crew violations of code of behaviour
	Build core competencies	Percentage implementation of training plan
		Retention rate of officers
		Retention rate of seafarers
	Advance IT	Number of new IT applications
		IT spending in dollars

Company F: Logistics service provider

Description

Company F is an international logistics company that has expanded globally over the last 20 years to become one of the world's leading logistics providers. It provides support to industry and trade in the global exchange of goods by providing land transport, worldwide air and ocean freight, contract logistics and supply chain management.

The company now operates from more than 2,000 locations worldwide and employs more than 80,000 people globally. The air and ocean freight divisions operate worldwide, whereas the land transport division operates on the European continent. In terms of air freight, it operates at more than 800 locations around the world and has 1,200 chartered flights each year with connecting hubs on all continents. The company facilitates the export of more than 1,300 thousand tons of air freight each year, and more than 2,200 thousand TEU. The company has about 750 warehouses worldwide and provides all types of business with logistics solutions for all kind of industries. Each week the company ships 32,000 truckloads. The company also delivers contract logistics and supply chain management. The provided services cover the entire spectrum of the value chain including procurement, production and distribution, to after-sales services.

The company provides an array of different logistics solutions that include:

- Road and rail land transport for the delivery of surface freight solutions
- Air freight with a global network and advanced logistics solutions
- Ocean freight that includes ships that carry thousands of containers a day to ports all around the world
- Contract logistics, the company being one of the leading and fastest-growing global logistics service providers
- Lead logistics products meaning that the customers' supply chain is optimized with the best service providers from start to finish.

Vision and mission

The company's vision is to be the leader in multi-modal transport and integrated logistics using cutting edge technology and innovative processes. The company seeks to offer to its customer base efficient logistics services using cutting edge technologies and to be highly competent and eventually become a strategic partner and contribute to managing their customers' supply chain.

The mission of the company is to provide value-added cost-effective supply chain solutions that would maximize customer satisfaction, achieve above-market returns, and become the employer of choice.

The strategic goals that can be derived from the vision and mission statements are as follows:

- Become the leader in multimodal-transport and leader in integrated logistics
- Achieve optimization of performance, transit times, productivity and efficiency
- Offer streamlined logistics services
- Use technology and continuously deploy innovation processes
- Be a highly competent and strategic partner
- Provide value-added and cost-effective supply chain solutions
- Maximize customer satisfaction
- Achieve above-market returns
- Become an employer of choice
- Be a sustainability leader
- Use innovation and digitalization to create value.

Strategy and KPIs

The strategy of the company is based on the achievement of economic, social and environmental goals in logistics and supply chain management. From an economic viewpoint, the company aims to be profitable but also to achieve leadership status in their target markets. The company aims to achieve long-term financial stability by investing in new and growing markets as well as through the development of the expertise of their human resources. To this end the company aims to be regarded as a leading employer that could attract people of all ages and professions from across the globe. They do so by offering employees local and international career opportunities and the prospect for internal development in the company's organizational ladder.

Furthermore, the company is looking to achieve long-term financial stability, by investing in new and growing markets. The company also aims to achieve customer satisfaction by delivering innovative services and solutions based on high performing processes and leading-edge information technology systems.

The company places considerable value on the issue of digitalization and the adoption of digital technologies to create value. The company focuses on the development of analytics and has invested in artificial intelligence and machine learning based solutions to facilitate improved customer service.

In terms of its environmental goals, the company aims to reduce their environmental footprint by developing an environmental sustainability strategy that encapsulates the reduction of external emissions from its logistics activities as well as energy efficient operations. The company was among the first to adopt environmental policies with specific goals and metrics across the whole spectrum of its operations. The strategic goals can be summarized as follows:

- Maintain profitable operations
- Be a quality leader
- Hold position as market leader
- Achieve long-term financial stability
- Invest in new markets
- Develop new businesses
- Nurture human resources
- Adopt innovative information technology systems
- Be an attractive employer
- Develop current employees
- Maintain green portfolio and eco-expertise
- Benchmark for carbon-emission
- Reduce all external emissions
- Achieve ESG leadership.

The main theme in the financial perspective is 'continuous improvement of financial performance'. Relevant goals that are stated or implied in the company's strategy include achieving profitability, be a market leader, invest in new markets, achieve efficiency improvements, management of cost structure and long-term financial stability. Relevant KPIs are developed in Table 7.6.

Based on the vision, mission and strategy goals of the company the fulfilment of the customer perspective objectives is centred around the environmental aspect, the service aspect and the creation of value for the customer.

CASE STUDIES OF MARITIME AND SHIPPING COMPANIES

Table 7.6 Global Logistics Service Provider – KPIs – Corporate Level

Perspective	Strategic goal	KPIs
Shareholder value	Increase profitability	Profit/loss before taxes on income
		EBITDA
		ROCE
		Net profit/loss for the year
	Financial stability	Working capital
		Cash flow from operating activities
		Equity
		Gross capital expenditures
	Cost control	Cost of financing
		Interest expenses
		Debt coverage
		Net financial debt
		Net capital expenditures
	Market share	Revenues
		Total assets
		Market share
Customer value	Increase customer value	Number of new services
		Number of new supply chains served
		Number of new system upgrades
	Customer satisfaction	Passengers (million)
		Customer retention rate
		Customer satisfaction index
		Net Promoter Score
		On-time delivery
		Punctuality
Internal processes	Improve environmental performance	Greenhouse gas emissions from operations
		Specific greenhouse gas emissions compared to previous period
		Share of renewable energies in the current mix
		Track kilometres noise remediated
		Energy Efficiency Existing Ship Index (EEXI) Carbon Intensity Index (CII)
	Create innovative solutions	Number of active projects per period
		Funds spend on innovation
		Revenue from new services
		Services introduced in the last year
		Number of employees in R&D

(*Continued*)

85

Table 7.6 (Continued)

Perspective	Strategic goal	KPIs
	Operations management effectiveness	Percentage within budget
		Percentage completed on time
		Capacity utilization rate
		Reduction in process waste level
		Time lost due to technical system failures
		Warehouse space contract logistics (million m²)
		Ocean freight volume (export) (thousand TEU
		Freight carried (million t)
		Volume sold (million pkm)
Learning and growth	Improve company culture and diversity	Share of women to men employed per period
		Employee satisfaction index
		Rate of men to women at managerial positions
	Improve employee skills	Dollars invested in training per period
		Number of training courses attended
	Reduce employee turnover	Employee satisfaction (index)
		Employee retention rate
	Technology	Number of new applications
		Number of new technology ventures announced per year
		Dollars invested in supply chain digitalization

The environmental aspect is one of the most prevalent in contemporary shipping and liner business mainly due to climate change and the enforcement of regulations that aim to reduce emissions in society. The company has ongoing goals in terms of reducing its gas emissions in the short, medium and longer term that go beyond the regulatory requirements.

The company recognizes that customer retention and customer satisfaction are based on the provision of high-quality service, creation of customer value and provision of safe, reliable, and punctual services in passenger and freight businesses. It has also been recognized that environmental performance is very important from the customer's point of view.

The company has several strategic goals that focus on the development and delivery of innovative services, efficient management of operations, development and adoption of new technologies and digitization in logistics.

From the key points highlighted in the vision, mission and strategy, a possible strategic theme for the company is also the improvement in company culture. The objectives of this perspective are to develop company employees by offering training and internal progression and invest in technology to achieve cost reduction and long-term financial stability.

Table 7.6 provides an illustration of the possible KPIs that can be adopted at corporate level for this company.

Company G: Dry bulk shipping company

Description

The company focuses on the operation of mainly Capesize dry bulk ships and is listed in the US capital markets. The company is incorporated in the Marshall Islands but has Greek ownership interests. The fleet of the company is relatively young with an average age of 10 years and total capacity of 18 million dwt Capesize vessels.

Vision and mission

The company's strategic vision is to position itself among the shipping industry's leaders in the dry bulk sector and generate shareholder value for the long term. It aspires to be a leading Capesize company with global operations and credible and sustainable services. The company's mission is to profit from positive long-term fundamentals in the dry bulk shipping industry. It aims to create value for shareholders though excellence in operations, safety and quality and promote high environmental, social and governance (ESG) values.

Strategy and KPIs

The company boasts a diverse customer base that includes large traders, cargo operators and miners, such as Rio Tinto, Cargill, Glencore, Trafigura, Vale, LDC, Anglo American, Oldendorff and Uniper among others. The company aims to create value by focusing on its reputation as a reliable operator, customer responsiveness, trustworthiness and integrity (i.e. the development of client relationships), high standards of safety and performance and operational reliability.

The company aims to track several critical performance variables including for the financial perspective growth and development of a modern fleet that is built almost exclusively in Japan and South Korea, a low average fleet age to ensure high performance and scrubber installation on ships in time charter contracts. The company aims to optimize its operating costs and control the vessel acquisition costs.

In its internal processes and systems, the company has invested in advanced technology (artificial intelligence and machine learning) to monitor fleet performance in real time, established internal control policies and procedures overseen by an experienced internal auditor and enhanced transparency through SEC and NASDAQ mandated financial reporting and disclosures.

In the customer perspective the company aims to develop long term customer relationships through responsiveness integrity and the trustworthiness of its people and be a reputable and reliable operator with high standards of performance and safety, adding value in every customer interaction and going beyond meeting its contractual commitments with high quality solutions and flexibility to yield added customer value. It aims to offer vessels of high quality and safety standards and provide first-class fleet operations that would result in competitive advantages to its charterers.

In terms of its learning and growth perspective the company has an experienced in-house team that closely monitors and supervises all key aspects of operations and the technical management of the fleet and a shipping committee to consider and vote upon all matters involving shipping and vessel finance. The main aim of the committee is to accelerate the pace of decision making in respect of shipping business opportunities, such as the acquisition of vessels or companies. Based on the aforementioned, a possible set of KPIs at corporate level would be as indicated in Table 7.7.

Table 7.7 Dry Bulk Company KPIs – Corporate Level

Perspective	Strategic goal	KPIs
Shareholder value	Cost reduction	Total cost percentage variance from budget
		Total cost as percentage of revenue
		OPEX cost variance from budget
	Revenue growth in a sustainable way	ROE
		ROIC
		Percentage of revenue from long-term charters
	Strong position in capesize segment	DWT of cargo transported
		Total cargo transported from capesizes
		Percentage of DWT capacity increase per year
	Financial performance	Percentage of leverage
		Percentage of equity raises
		Number of years of active involvements
		Cost of financing
Customer value	Customer relationship	Customer Satisfaction Index
		Customer Service Rating Index
		Number of reported charterers' complaints
	Customer business development	Number of contracts with new charterers
		Charterers retention rate
		Number of charterparties per charterer

	Customer loyalty	Charterer retention rate
		Number of charterparties per charterer
		Leading charterers retention rate
Internal processes	Employee satisfaction	Employee Satisfaction Index
		Employee retention rate
		Number of reported complaints
	Environental preservation and sustainability	Percentage of emissions reduction (CO_2, Sox, Nox)
		Energy consumption/Ton-mile
		Energy Efficiency Existing Ship Index (EEXI)
		Carbon Intensity Index (CII)
	Improve quality	Percentage of goals achieved per department
		Percentage of issues resolved per department
		Number of ISO certifications
		Number of safety training programs and drills
		Safety Index
Learning and Growth	Training of employees	Hours of training per employee per hour
		Employee Training Practicability Index
		Percentage of acceptable training scores
	Innovative technology adoption	Capital investment in innovative technological solutions
		Technology Assimilation Rating Index
	Governance	Number of internal audit observations
		Number of internal audits
		Rate of shipping committee decisions implementation
	Environmental management	Number of new environmental initiatives
		Number of new partnerships In environmental projects

Bibliography

Christiansen, M., Hellsten, E., Pisinger, D., Sacramento, D., and Vilhelmsen, C. (2020). Liner shipping network design. *European Journal of Operational Research*, 286(1), pp. 1–20.

Gibson, M., Murphy, A. J., and Pazouki, K. (2019). Evaluation of environmental performance indices for ships. *Transportation Research Part D: Transport and Environment*, 73, pp. 152–161.

Heij, C., and Knapp, S. (2012). Evaluation of safety and environmental risk at individual ship and company level. *Transportation Research Part D: Transport and Environment*, 17(3), pp. 228–236.

Joseph, G. (2009). Mapping, measurement and alignment of strategy using the balanced scorecard: The Tata steel case. *Accounting Education*, 18(2), pp. 117–130.

Kanamoto, K., Murong, L., and Nakashima, M. (2021). Can maritime big data be applied to shipping industry analysis? Focussing on commodities and vessel sizes of dry bulk carriers. *Maritime Economics and Logistics*, 23, pp. 211–236.

Kyprianidou, I., Worrell, E., and Charalambides, G. A. (2021). The cost-effectiveness of CO2 mitigation measures for the decarbonisation of shipping. The case study of a globally operating ship-management company. *Journal of Cleaner Production*, 316, pp. 1–20.

Lyridis, D. V., and Papaleonidas, C. (2019). Organization and management of tanker shipping companies. In Panayides, Ph. M. (ed) *The Routledge Handbook of Maritime Management*, 1st ed., pp. 58–79. London: Routledge.

Park, S., Lee, H., and Chae, S. W. (2017). Rethinking balanced scorecard (BSC) measures: Formative versus reflective measurement models. *International Journal of Productivity and Performance Management*, 66(1), pp. 92–110.

Poulsen, R. T., Viktorelius, M., Varvne, H., Rasmussen, H. B., and von Knorring, H. (2022). Energy efficiency in ship operations – Exploring voyage decisions and decision-makers. *Transportation Research Part D: Transport and Environment*, 102, pp. 103–120.

Poulsen, T. T., Ponte, S., van Leeuwen, J., and Rehmatulla, N. (2021). The potential and limits of environmental disclosure regulation: A global value chain perspective applied to tanker shipping. *Global Environmental Politics*, 21(2), pp. 99–120.

Romano, A., and Yang, Z. (2022). *Decarbonisation of Shipping: A State of the Art Survey for 2000–2020*. Amsterdam: Elsevier Science Direct.

Siddiqui, A. W., and Verma, M. (2018). Assessing risk in the intercontinental transportation of crude oil. *Maritime Economics & Logistics*, 20, pp. 280–299.

CHAPTER 8

Department performance in shipping and transportation

Introduction

The development of an effective performance management system requires that each business unit or department create their own strategy map. Department strategy maps must incorporate department goals which in turn should be measured by relevant key performance indicators (KPIs). In developing a system to evaluate shipping company department performance it is important to recognize the business processes and activities that take place at the department level within the shipping organization as well as the ensuing organizational structure. This chapter provides a brief overview of department functions before explaining the process of cascation and the development of goals and Key Performance Indicators at department level to ensure link and integration with those at corporate level.

Typical departments and functions in maritime organizations

The most typical departments in shipping or ship operating companies include among others:

- Operations and post fixture department
- Technical department
- Crew department
- Chartering or commercial department
- Quality safety and environmental management department
- Business development or marketing department
- Accounting and finance department
- Procurement and purchasing department

The operations department is responsible for the daily running of the ship including ship-shore communication, port agent appointment, advance payments, bunker supplier selection, order placement and bunkers delivery. Supplies, spare parts and other consumables are supplied through a process of ordering and approving by the technical department in collaboration with the procurement/purchasing department that places the orders and is responsible for supplier, selection, goods delivery, procurement and invoice processing.

DOI: 10.4324/9781315717845-8   91

The technical department approves the quality of the ordered materials and parts and is also engaged in the maintenance of the technical seaworthiness and cargo-worthiness of the vessels as well as with shipyard selection and repairs and maintenance supervision.

The crew department is responsible for crew recruitment and crew management which mainly includes seafarers hiring, training and evaluation, payroll of seafarers, medical, travel and repatriation arrangements. The human resource department is also responsible for shore personnel hiring, payroll, terminating, salary changes, employee bonus, leaving indemnity, stock incentive plan, monthly payroll including monthly wages and social security payments.

The chartering department may also be referred to as the commercial department and is responsible for finding, negotiating and securing employment for the ships on voyage and time charters. The department may also be responsible and undertake post-fixture work which includes the arrangement and monitoring of financial transactions such as freight, hire and demurrage payments, invoicing and liaison in the payment of brokerage and other chartering related commissions.

The accounting and financial department is responsible for the preparation of accounts and budgets as well as liaison with banks, financial institutions, payments and fund transfer, preparation of loan proposals and annual reports monitoring budgets, bank reconciliation, invoice processing, accounting treatment including accruals and amortization, foreign currency, dividends, capital markets, and monitoring of accounting policies.

The insurance and claims department is responsible for the arrangement of insurance including marine insurance such as Hull and Machinery (H&M), Protection and Indemnity (P&I) as well as FD&D, claims management and processing of claims collection.

Other support departments such as information systems cover automated processes and controls to implement the financial, operational and compliance business objectives, and safeguarding of company's assets.

In developing their strategy map and performance management goals and KPIs, the aim of departments should be focused on answering two key questions:

1. How will the department help the organization to execute its strategy?
2. Which objectives and KPIs are relevant to the department that will integrate into the cause and effect strategy map of the company?

Department key performance indicators should not be more than 20 to 30 in number. In addition, the development of KPIs at lower levels such as for units, sub-units or team level (e.g. fleets in ship management companies) should not be more than about 10 to 15 KPIs per unit, and five KPIs per sub-unit.

The process of integrating department goals and KPIs to the strategy map of the company (corporate scorecard) is the process of cascation.

Developing departmental objectives and KPIs:
The cascation process

The identification of objectives begins by defining best practices in the context of company functions. The delineation of functions and what would be regarded as best practice is fundamental to the development of goals as well as key performance indicators at department level.

The top-down approach that is suggested in the development of the performance management system enables the alignment of corporate goals with department and lower-level team (e.g. fleet) goals and objectives. The objective of an organization-wide performance management system is to link the strategy manifested in the mission, vision and strategic goals to the work that people do in departments and teams. In this way people at lower levels know and understand how they contribute to higher level desired results and become strategy-focused.

Cascading the balanced scorecard is therefore the process by which corporate-wide goals are translated and aligned to departments goals and support unit or team goals. As corporate goals are cascaded down the organizational hierarchy, they become more operational and tactical. Performance measures (KPIs) are also aligned, and at lower levels they are also more operational. This instils organization-wide consistency and focus and enables communication of results across all levels. This alignment step is critical to becoming a strategy-focused organization.

A strategy map should clearly depict the relationship between corporate level goals and objectives and those of departments and teams. In the same way that KPIs at higher levels have owners and accountability is fostered, so do KPIs at lower levels. Since scorecards are used to improve performance and accountability it is also important to incentivize the elicitation of the desired employee behaviours through recognition and rewards.

In a typical cascation process, the corporate scorecard will form the starting point. Cascation will involve the selection of a particular objective that exists within one of the perspectives of the corporate balanced scorecard and link that one to a relevant objective at the lower (e.g. department) level. So for instance at the corporate level in the internal process perspective the objective innovation effectiveness may be measured by the 'new product contribution to revenues' (KPI) at the business unit level in the internal process perspective the objective innovation effectiveness may be measured by the 'number of new products introduced successfully in a year' (KPI), whereas in the new product development department scorecard (3rd tier cascation) in the internal process perspective the objectives may include 'pipeline management' and 'efficient operation' and relevant measures would be 'average products in the pipeline' and 'average time to launch' (KPIs).

It must be pointed out that much of the internal process related work normally takes place at department level, therefore more KPI related performance measures will inevitably precipitate.

Operations department objectives and KPIs

The operations department monitors the fleet's performance and oversees the needs of the ship while at sea or in port. The operations department is responsible for providing solutions to all the problems that may arise and may impede the smooth operation of the vessels. The operations department is responsible for overseeing that ships are seamlessly integrated into the management operations of the company, that the right personnel is allocated for monitoring ship operations, that the ship is available at the right place and time to undertake the assigned operations and that the ship is ready for certification and for trading in all respects and purposes.

This is achieved by maintaining continuous communication with the ships and agents and taking all appropriate activities according to their needs. The operations department works closely with other departments of the company. For example, it works closely with finance and accounts because it supervises the disbursements of all funds necessary to run the ships in close cooperation with the purchasing and supply department and monitors the daily operating costs of the fleet. The operations department ensures that all vessels are provided with the necessary stores, provisions and spare parts. In addition, it ensures that the crew has all necessary facilities and equipment required for safe operations and that the quality control systems are upheld.

Ship operation performance is imperative and best practice in technical management requires the ability to comply with the IMO's Ship Energy Efficiency Management Plan (SEEMP). Steps taken to achieve efficient operation of the ship under SEEMP are speed optimization, weather routing, hull monitoring and maintenance, efficient cargo operation and electric power management. SEEMP is basically monitoring carried out by shore staff which collects the data from the ship via the use of sensors, AIS, logbooks and satellite records.

Best practices in purchasing span the delivery of provisions and bunkers, the adoption of proactive actions and close communication with the ship's captain and in efficiently arranging freight, hire and demurrage collection.

Table 8.1 Operations Department's Goals and KPIs

Perspective	Strategy goal	KPIs
Financial	Cost	Bunker fuel cost optimization
		Port cost percentage deviation from estimate
	Financial reliability	Percentage variation from budget
		Cost compare to industry average
		Freight compared to industry average
Customer	Operational reliability	Number of off-hire days for time-chartered ships per period
		Number of technical problems leading to off-hire per period
		Level of hire deductions from customers
		Number of customer complaints

DEPARTMENT PERFORMANCE IN SHIPPING AND TRANSPORTATION

Perspective	Strategy goal	KPIs
Internal process	Port agent liaison	Number of agent communication
		Number of port agent problems recorded per period
	Voyage optimization	Number of ballast days
		Average port waiting hours
		Total hours deviation from ETA
		Percentage of delayed arrivals
	Operational reliability	Number of off-hire days for time-chartered ships per period
		Number of technical problems leading to off-hire per period
		Number of conditions of class
		Number of environmental related deficiencies
		Number of failures of critical equipment and systems
		Number of cargo spillage incidents
		Number of observations during commercial inspections
		Planned unavailability
	Ship-shore communication	Number of recorded problems
		Number of times instructions not followed
Learning and growth	Energy efficiency	Energy Efficiency Existing Ship Index (EEXI)
	Environmental operations	Environmental Ship Index
		Carbon Intensity Index (CII)

Technical department objectives and KPIs

Technical operations management includes activities required to maintain a ship in a safe, seaworthy and operationally reliable condition, meeting all required international and national legislation, to carry out the prime objective which is the safe and efficient carriage of cargo.

The technical department is charged with all matters that involve the proper maintenance of the fleet's vessels. It ensures that the engine room and deck machinery and equipment run smoothly and stay problem-free, schedules their maintenance, supplies (in direct co-operation with the procurement and purchasing department) the necessary spare parts and supervises dry-dockings and other repairs.

Together with the operations department, it is also responsible for the renewal of all ship certificates whenever necessary, for reviewing technical reports, and appraising the overall performance of the engines. The main activities include the preparation and implementation of the company's Safety Management System (SMS) as required by the International Maritime Organization (IMO) and particularly the

95

International Safety Management Code (ISM Code), International Organization for Standardization (ISO) and other key stakeholders, such as classification societies and charterers. In addition, the department is involved in the establishment and diligent application of a ship asset preservation and maintenance programme that encompasses all ships' machinery, equipment and structure and the implementation of a procurement system that provides ships with provisions, spare parts and stores in accordance with the needs of the crew, the maintenance programme and the ship's operations. In addition, the department has the responsibility of maintaining a clear and transparent monitoring and reporting system that provides management information, covering the key areas of ship operation, including safety performance; ship condition, reliability and maintenance status; budget variance; ship certificate status; oil major vetting and port state control performance; ship emissions, environmental compliance and energy efficiency. It is also responsible for implementing the ship's planned maintenance programme, identifying critical equipment, managing modifications and upgrades, and dry docking and afloat repairs.

Technical management best management practices include the development of an electronic planned maintenance system that will enable centralized control of the maintenance programme through relevant databases and scheduling across the fleet. This will facilitate the achievement of economies of scale in ship maintenance and will create synergies. The maintenance plan requires the improvement of hull maintenance effectiveness through systematic inspections and efficient hull coating programmes. In addition, best practices entail the development of dedicated dry-docking teams to oversee dry docking operations and the development of particular competencies.

Based on the previous discussion the technical department's goals and relevant KPIs can be formulated as in Table 8.2.

Table 8.2 Sample of Technical Department's Goals and KPIs

Perspective	Strategy goal	KPIs
Financial	Dry-docking	Actual drydocking costs
		Actual drydocking duration
		Actual unavailability
		Agreed drydocking budget
		Agreed drydocking duration
Customer	Technical conformance	Number of navigational related deficiencies
		Number of operational related deficiencies
		Number of conditions of class
		Number of environmental related deficiencies
		Number of health and safety related deficiencies
		Number of PSC deficiencies
		Number of PSC detentions

Perspective	Strategy goal	KPIs
Internal process	Reduce failures	Number of ballast water management violations
		Number of cargo related incidents
		Number of failures of critical equipment and systems
		Number of security related deficiencies
	Internal evaluation	Number of observations during commercial inspections
		Planned unavailability
Learning and growth	External evaluation	Number of PSC inspections
		Number of PSC inspections resulting in zero deficiencies
		Number of recorded external inspections
		Number of commercial inspections

Crewing department objectives and KPIs

One of the core departments in ship operations management is the crewing department. The goals of the crewing department are to recruit competent and qualified crew cost-efficiently and to train, retain and manage the crew. Best practices of the crew department include:

- Recruit qualified personnel
- Increase access to new crew
- Use technology for crew training (e.g. bridge and engine simulators)
- Develop attractive crew remuneration and leave packages
- Develop crew development pathways
- Improve crew welfare practices such as ease of communication, access to on-board internet etc.
- Train and develop crew competencies including language
- Increase officer and crew retention
- Improve crew information quality
- Develop crew appraisal systems
- Improve the quality of the work environment
- Use state of the art technology for crew matters

Developing goals and KPIs for the crew department begins with the cascading process considering the corporate goals and critical success factors that are relevant to the crew department. Such goals may include a focus on costs (overhead and operating costs), safety and ship availability.

In terms of the cost equation, the reduction of the overhead costs will be a goal relevant to the shareholder perspective whereas crew cost reduction (or optimization) will be relevant to the customer perspective in the scorecard strategy map of the crew department. The scope of the crew department is mainly focused on crew recruitment and crew management and relevant goals may be developed within the internal process perspective. In terms of crew recruitment, crew departments may focus on three key goals that will be depicted on their strategy maps, viz., 'increase access to new crew', 'recruit quality crew' and 'optimize/minimize crewing time'.

On this basis the KPIs used to measure the three goals may be as depicted in Table 8.3:

Table 8.3 Crewing Goals and KPIs for Crew Department

Perspective	*Strategy goal*	*KPIs*
Financial	Crewing cost	Average salary
		Average salary for all employees reporting to the selected manager
		Average sourcing cost per hire
		Average training costs per employee
		Compensation cost as a percentage of revenue
		HR department cost per FTE
		Cost per hire
		Return on investment (ROI) of training
		Internal, external, and total headcount recruiting costs and ratios
		Actual versus budgeted cost of hire
		Average interviewing costs
Customer	Increase access to new crew	Number of new partnerships with crewing agencies
		Number of new partnerships with marine academies
		Average number of cadets on board
		Number of seafarers not relieved on time
		Time to fill
		Average months placement
		Staffing efficiency
Internal process	Recruit quality crew	Number of early terminations
		New crew hired quality
		HR average years of service (incumbents)
		HR average years of service (terminations)
		Percentage of new hire retention
		Number of cases with medical problems undetected
		Number of unqualified personnel introduced by agents
		Number of dismissed crew, average years of crew experience
		Number of cadets under training with the DOC holder
		Number of officers onboard
		Number of charges of criminal offences
		Number of cases where drugs or alcohol is abused
		Number of violations of rest hours

DEPARTMENT PERFORMANCE IN SHIPPING AND TRANSPORTATION

Perspective	Strategy goal	KPIs
Learning and growth	Improve response	Number of delays due to crew
		Average time to crew a vessel
	Increase officer retention	Number of months working with company
		Number of officers employed
		Number of dismissals
		Number of officer terminations
		Average time employees are in same job/function
		Average length of service of all current employees
	Safety awareness	Number of trainings attended
		Number of fatalities due to work injuries
		Number of fatalities due to sickness
		Number of logged warnings
		Number of HR related deficiencies
		Number of cases where drugs or alcohol is abuse
	Crew satisfaction	Change in satisfaction index per period surveyed
		Number of HR related deficiencies
		Total overtime hours as a percentage of all work hours
	New skills for officers	Number of trainings attended
		Number of officer trainee man days
		Ratio of internal versus external training
		Number of cadets under training with the ship manager
		Average number of officers employed
		Number of officer trainee man days
		Number of officers onboard
		Average number of training hours per employee
		Training penetration rate (percentage of employees completing a course compared to all FTEs)
	Improve human resource quality	Number of dismissed crew
		Number of seafarers not relieved on time
		Number of charges of criminal offences
		Number of lost workday cases
		Number of absconded crew
		Number of cases where a crew member is sick for more than 24 hours
		Number of cases where drugs or alcohol is abused
		Number of violations of rest hours
		Annualized voluntary employee turnover rate
		Average performance scores of departing seafarers
		Average time to competence

(*Continued*)

Table 8.3 (Continued)

Perspective	Strategy goal	KPIs
	Quality of work environment	Quality of Work Environment Index
		Number of violations of rest hours
		Number of officer terminations from whatever cause
		Number of lost workday cases
		Number of absconded crew
		Number of cases where a crew member is sick for more than 24 hours
	Improve crew information quality	Number of records in error
		Average time to update employee records
	Foster business focus culture	Number of incidents
		Number of HR related deficiencies
		Number of officer terminations from whatever cause

The first three KPIs reflect the ability of the company to increase access to new crew. However, apart from recruiting new crew efficiently, the department must ensure that the crew is of high quality. In this context another key goal is the recruitment of quality crew and relevant KPIs are shown in the Table 8.3.

In terms of crew management, the goals of the department at the internal process perspective are to increase officer retention, raise crew safety awareness, achieve crew satisfaction, incorporate new skills for officers and improve the quality of the work environment.

As crew departments are principally engaged with crew recruitment and crew management, a department may be structured into sub-divisions that will be responsible for the two main tasks respectively. On this basis, there might be further cascation from the crew department to the sub-division or team level. The cascation entails further break down of goals and KPIs. For instance, if in the process perspective a goal of the crew department is to 'recruit quality crew' (KPI: Number of early terminations) then an aligned goal may be found at the sub-division or crew recruitment team level. Hence at the crew recruitment team the goal would be 'effective recruitment process' and KPIs may include 'number of non-competent personnel recruited', 'number of personnel with medical problems undetected' and 'change in number of unqualified personnel introduced by agencies'.

Chartering department objectives and KPIs

Companies in the business of maritime transportation range from specialized shipping entities to shipping pools and parts of large shipping conglomerates. The task of the business entity is to serve the needs of charterers wishing to transport cargoes and commodities.

Be it a specialized shipping company with a fleet of different types of carriers or a more specialized shipping pool with a specific non-diversified ship type mixture, it is imperative for chartering and charter party post fixture performance to be measured and monitored.

To manage and improve the performance of the chartering department or chartering unit within a company, there must be a performance management system to facilitate the following management tasks:

1. Enable the setting of realistic chartering targets
2. Track chartering performance
3. Identify chartering performance limitations
4. Identify achievement of chartering performance targets
5. Communicate chartering performance internally and where relevant externally
6. Provide the basis for continuous improvement of chartering practice
7. Identify the contribution of chartering specific ship types to profitability.

In measuring chartering performance, the starting point would be to consider the corporate or business level objectives of the organization. The mission and vision statements as well as the corporate objectives stated by publicly traded dry bulk shipping companies are centred on certain main key objectives which include:

- Profitability and contribution to revenues
- Stability of income, increased revenue and shareholder satisfaction
- Productivity and reduction of voyage and operating expenses
- Satisfaction, confidence and trust of customers
- Long-term customer relationships and ship utilization
- Confidence of financial institutions towards the company (banks, investors, funds)
- Quality and efficiency in ship management and shipping operations
- Health, safety and the environment
- Employee competence and satisfaction
- Technology and innovation

On this basis the department responsible for the chartering function will need to concentrate on four broad areas in order to achieve maximum contribution towards the corporate level goals.

The four areas entail (1) the ability of chartering to contribute to the company's financial goals; (2) whether charterers (customers) are satisfied with the charters, the chartering process, and charter party performance (post fixture); (3) whether there are effective and efficient internal processes for achieving chartering goals and charter party performance; and (4) whether the company continuously invests in innovative technological systems and the training and development of human resources to achieve chartering goals. It is imperative that the professionals engaged in chartering operations are able and committed to finding optimal solutions to the transportation requirements of the customer based on integrity and real engagement.

The aim of the chartering or commercial department is to locate the most suitable business of the ships and negotiate the best freight and hire rates with the respective charterers. This is done through maintenance of relationships with existing clients and with shipbrokers.

Financial goals and KPIs of the chartering department

In terms of the financial goals of chartering they relate directly to the goals of the corporation and include contribution to revenue, reduction (optimization) of operating and voyage costs, stability of income, profitability, ship/asset productivity (utilization) and competitive benchmarking.

The contribution of chartering to the financial perspective utilizes KPIs mainly from the accounting and finance literature and from the financial statements of the companies. It makes use of measures such as profitability, return on equity (ROE), return on assets (ROA), and return on investment (ROI), as well as costs (fixed operating costs and variable voyage costs). It may also be beneficial to benchmark rates of all fixtures against an index that corresponds to the ship being chartered (e.g. Panamax, Supramax etc.) to reveal performance against the market and deviations from the index. This may be done on a monthly basis for time series analysis.

On this basis the KPIs used to measure the chartering department's goals and KPIs at the shareholder value perspective could be as shown in Table 8.4.

Table 8.4 Chartering Department Financial Perspective Goals and KPIs

Perspective	Strategy goal	KPIs
Shareholder value	Profitability margin per charter	Percentage deviation from estimate
		Bunker fuel cost optimization
		Port cost percentage deviation from estimate
		Absolute profitability from chartering
		Number of fixtures concluded per year
	Chartering effectiveness	Percentage voyage charters fulfilled without problems
		Percentage time charters fulfilled without problems
	Chartering productivity	Time charters contribution to revenue (time charters contribution to profit)
		Voyage charters contribution to revenue (voyage charters contribution to profit)
		Number of time charters (duration) concluded/time t
		Number of voyage charters (duration) concluded/time t

The main issues that are relevant to this perspective are profitability, productivity, optimization, and effectiveness. A fundamental objective of any company is of course profitability. Shipping companies should measure the extent to which their core functions (the chartering and operation of their ships) contribute to company profitability. Absolute profitability may be measured as well as the percent deviation from an estimated profitability, measured quarterly or on a yearly basis in accordance with the financial statements. Ultimately, profitability will also be reflected in the number of concluded fixtures, which represents another KPI that may be tracked.

The KPI bunker fuel cost optimization measures the deviation from a forecasted estimate of the ability of the organization to optimize bunker fuel cost. Optimization is used instead of bunker cost reduction due to the necessity of considering market conditions. Hence, when the cost of oil is rising, then one would expect bunker fuel cost to also rise. However, what is important is the ability to keep bunker fuel costs stable or rising at a lower rate relative to the price of crude oil or the industry average price for bunker costs.

Port costs vary depending on the port and the method it adopts to levy charges as well as the rates charged. Port costs also vary depending on the type of services rendered, days spent in port etc., so on this basis, it would be highly unlikely that benchmarks among different ports will reveal particularly meaningful measurements. A rational way of measuring and managing this type of cost would be to benchmark against a predetermined estimate. The percentage deviation from a port cost estimate for a given port or ports would be useful feedback that could be used for improvement, including port cost reduction or port cost optimization.

Another relevant KPI for chartering productivity measures the number of time charters of a specified duration (e.g. one year) that have been agreed during a specified time period that could be monthly, quarterly, or yearly. It reflects the ability of the chartering department or that of the company to attract charterers, finalize negotiations, and conclude fixture agreements.

A similar KPI is the number of voyage charters (duration) concluded in a time period t and is similar to the previous one but refers to voyage charters instead of time charters. The KPI time charters contribution to revenue (or alternatively time charters contribution to profit) is important for corporate-level decision makers interested in analyzing the contribution of time charters to revenue or profit. At first instance the contribution of time charters to revenue may be measured, and this is an important indicator in the context of pursuing time charters. However, what might be of real importance is the extent to which time charters contribute to profit. This may be expressed as a percentage of total profit emanating from time chartering ships over a specified period of time (quarterly or yearly).

In the context of voyage chartering a relevant KPI measures the contribution of voyage charters to revenue (or alternatively voyage charters contribution to profit), Chartering effectiveness measures the percentage of voyage charters fulfilled without problems with a relevant KPI. The KPI measures the ability of the chartering department to fulfil all obligations arising from a voyage chartering agreement without any problems during the period of the voyage charter. A similar KPI to the previous one, but this time to measure the ability of the chartering department to fulfil obligations under time charters without problems.

The KPI vessel utilization rate (actual number of days chartered to total days available for charter) measures the ability to fully utilize the main assets of the company (i.e., the ships), thus reflecting directly chartering effectiveness.

Customer goals of the chartering department

Customer goals represent an important area for performance measurement for the chartering entity. Financial goals will not be achieved without satisfying the needs of customers. The customers may be long-term customers or in the spot market. Their needs include fundamental needs such as the fulfilment of transportation requirements cost-efficiently, safely with high quality and environmentally friendly transportation solutions but also the ability to provide flexible solutions to long-term customers, the development of long-term relationships, maintenance of relations with shippers and receivers, development of transportation programmes to fit the customers' production schedules and storage capacities for long term customers. The customer perspective focuses on the aspects of performance that are considered important from the charterer's point of view. These would invariably include aspects relevant to the pre-fixture as well as post-fixture performance. Hence, aspects such as arrival within laycan, on-time delivery, speed, and consumption warranties would be imperative and very relevant for inclusion in this perspective.

KPIs in the context of two themes, voyage charters and time charters, are relevant for this perspective. Vessels under voyage charter should arrive at the port of loading during the period of time defined in the laycan clause. Any delay beyond the laycan deadline may have serious repercussions for the shipowner that may even go as far as the cancelling of the charter party contract. On this basis it is important to keep track of the number of times the laycan period has been missed during a defined period of time (e.g. quarterly). Obviously, the target for this KPI should be zero. In addition, if missed laycans have resulted in voyage charter cancellations, then this should be recorded and gauged in an appropriate KPI.

If a NOR is invalid or 'not true', then this will lead to potential delay at the expense of the shipowner. It is important that NOR is always true and given when the ship is ready to receive cargo with clean-swept holds and ready for ordinary cargo service. A target of zero should be set when measuring the number of times that an invalid NOR has been issued.

The number of laytime delays arising from owners' fault is an aggregate KPI that reflects the ability of the company to ensure that laytime operations commence and finish within the timelines set. In order to establish time-related performance targets it is important that relevant KPIs measure the days, hours and minutes of laytime delay. A record of laytime delays that have arisen due to owners' fault must be kept. This KPI may be measured as the number of such laytime delays, but an associated KPI may measure such delays in terms of days, hours, and minutes of delay.

Timeliness is fundamental to voyage charter parties, and on-time arrival at the port of discharge is a measure that needs to be tracked. Relevant KPIs include the number of times that the vessel has arrived late and in a time charter context, the number of times that the ship has not been delivered on time. Another relevant KPI could be the number or laycan cancellations effected for time and voyage charters. Even a single delay in time charter vessel delivery due to owner's fault would fall outside the target of any shipping or ship operating company. The KPIs are therefore fundamental to the achievement of a key requirement in chartering: that is, the delivery of the ship on time, in a time charter agreement. It is an absolute obligation undertaken by the shipowner to provide a ship that is seaworthy and that includes the capability to sail at the speeds agreed to in the charter party, although half a knot leeway may be acceptable. If the ship does not attain the stipulated speed in accordance with the terms of the charter party, the charterer may bring a claim for unseaworthiness and loss of time arising from it.

With respect to speed and consumption specifications, the KPI would be the number of deviations from the speed and consumption specifications indicated in the charter party. Another key objective is off-hire (or rather its minimization). Off-hire may arise from a number of reasons related to the seaworthiness of the ship and reflects operational reliability. It is an important KPI for the chartering department as well as other departments, since each off-hire day represents lost revenue for the shipowner. The number of days off-hire is a critical KPI for the chartering operations.

If a vessel goes off-hire, the charterers may be entitled to deduct hire. This right arises either contractually or by means of the principle of equitable set-off. An aggregate number of deductions from hire may be estimated or the total sum of deducted hire in US dollars per time period, which probably represents a more relevant and accurate KPI.

The objective 'human resource (HR) compliance to charter party' can be measured using the KPI of number of incidents of noncompliance which measures directly the ability of HR to fully comply with the terms of the charter party.

Based on the previous discussion Table 8.5 illustrates that possible goals and KPIs of the chartering department from a customer's value perspective.

Internal process goals of the chartering department

The internal process perspective focuses on those aspects of performance that are critical to the success of an organization and reside in the effectiveness and efficiency of processes and operations within the organization. Relevant KPIs for this perspective should measure issues such as the ability to identify cargo owners quickly, the ability to respond to orders on time, the speed and efficiency within which chartering negotiations are concluded, etc.

Table 8.5 Chartering Department Customer Perspective Goals and KPIs

Perspective	Strategy goal	KPIs
Customer value	On time lay can (voyage charter)	Number of times not arrived on time
		Average lay can delay
	Notice of readiness	Number of times NOR is invalid
		Number of time NOR is late
		Number of times NOR is not true
	Laytime delays due to owner's fault (voyage charter)	Number of laytime delays
		Days, hours and minutes of laytime delay
		Number of times of late arrival
	No time port of discharge arrival (voyage charter)	Number of times of late arrival
		Average delay
	On time delivery (time charter)	Number of times not delivered on time
		Average delay
	Speed and consumption specs	Number of deviations from charter party on speed
		Number of deviations from charter party on consumption
		Average consumption deviation per voyage
		Average speed deviation per voyage
	Off-hire	Number of off-hire days
		Amount of off-hire claims
	Deductions from hire	Number of times charterers deducted hire
		Total in US dollars deducted from hire
	HR compliance to CP	Number of times of non-compliance
		Number of non-compliance claims
		Non-compliance claims payable per period

This perspective focuses on the effectiveness of voyage charters, claims processes, and processes for payment of freight and hire. In the context of voyage charter effectiveness, it is important to measure the ability of the company to conclude fixtures and chartering deals. This can be measured by such KPIs as the number of positions per period to total number of ships available, or the number of positions communicated. The indicators assess the extent to which the chartering department is able to provide a given number of positions for the available ships per specific time period. For a chartering department to be productive, it must be able to convey information as to vessel availability efficiently; hence, this KPI will provide an assessment to this extent. Data can be collected directly from the chartering department on a daily basis. The company may set a certain target for this KPI at a level that it will consider adequate, given the number of ships available.

A shipping company may enter the charter with relevant positions that will ultimately lead to the conclusion of a fixture. During the negotiations process positions and offers may or may not always materialize into firm offers or even agreement of the charter arrangement. A shipping company may gauge various relevant metrics in this context and should be able to assess the efficiency with which positions are turned into firm offers. Hence, it would be important to determine the number of firm offers made per time period in relation to the ships that are available and under negotiation. Another KPI also measures the number of firm offers to total fixtures agreed, measuring effectiveness in turning firm offers into fixtures.

The voyage estimation aims to calculate in advance the profit or loss that will accrue to the shipowner from the specific voyage in question. Various assumptions will be encapsulated in the voyage estimation, and the process itself will follow specific routines. In order to determine the analyst's ability to execute realistic and accurate voyage estimations it is important to compare the results of the voyage estimate and the budgeted costs against the actual costs after the conclusion of every chartering fixture. This will measure the ability of the analyst to perform accurate voyage estimation but also serves as a method for improving performance. The estimation should be checked against the realized profit or loss and any deviations from the estimated sum should be acknowledged and, where necessary, process improvements should be adopted. The number of process improvements per time period reflects the company's ability to acknowledge limitations and also record the improvement action that has been taken.

Chartering effectiveness may also be measured by the number of demurrage or dispatch claims, as higher levels of demurrage or dispatch will point to the inefficiency in agreeing and executing the right terms in the fixtures.

On this basis the KPIs used to measure the chartering department's goals and KPIs at the internal process perspective could be as shown in Table 8.6.

Claims resolution is an important goal for the commercial or chartering department. The objective is to resolve claims amicably but also to resolve them as quickly as possible. On this basis relevant KPIs measure the average time to resolve a claim out of total claims in a time period. The objective is to minimize this time in so far as practicable. Another KPI may measure the number of claims that are resolved amicably in relation to the total claims per time period.

Regarding the receipt of freight and hire this is measured for voyage charters and time charters respectively. The KPIs measure the number of times freight/hire is delayed by gauging the number of times that charterers have not fulfilled their absolute obligation to pay freight and the duration of the delay (in days). Average delay (days) of freight payment measures the ability of the company to receive cash due from the charter of its fleet of ships. Any delays in the payment of freight must be recorded.

Table 8.6 Chartering Department Internal Process Perspective Goals and KPIs

Perspective	Strategy goal	KPIs
Internal processes	Chartering effectiveness	Number of positions per day
		Number of firm offers per day
		Number of firm offers per time period in relation to available ships
		Number of firm offers to total fixtures agreed per time period
		Demurrage claims in US dollars per time period
		Dispatch claims in US dollars per time period
	Voyage estimating performance	Number of voyage estimation process improvements per time period
		Accuracy of voyage estimating vis-a-vis actual voyage costs
	Claims resolution	Number of claims resolved amicably
		Average time to resolve a claim
	Receipt of freight/hire	Number of times freight/hire is delayed
		Average delay (days) of freight payment (voyage charter)
		Average delay (days) of hire payment (time charter)
	Demurrage or dispatch claims	Number of demurrage claims per period
		Amount of demurrage/dispatch claims (absolute number of claims per time period or amount in US dollars) per time t

Learning, growth, innovation goals and KPIs for chartering

Finally, the fourth area termed the innovation and growth perspective focuses on measuring performance and ability to develop human and technological resources that are relevant and lead to improvement of chartering practice. This area focuses on the competence of the human resources and other resources that can be utilized in the context of chartering, such as information technology.

The experience of chartering personnel may be gauged by directly investigating the average number of years of shipping experience and the number of years in the department. The results would be aggregated.

Qualification of chartering personnel can be monitored by using the KPI 'number of personnel with chartering qualifications'. The measure represents a reflection of the personnel with specialized chartering qualifications and may include academic as well as professional qualifications in chartering and maritime business. Training of chartering personnel may also be gauged by the number of training programmes completed per year and the average spending on training per person per year. The KPIs reflect the training received by personnel specific to the chartering process.

Table 8.7 Chartering Department Learning and Growth Perspective Goals and KPIs

Perspective	Strategy goal	KPIs
Learning and growth	Chartering personnel experience	Average shipping experience in number of years
		Number of years in the department
	Qualifications	Number of personnel with chartering qualifications
		Number of training programs completed per year
	Training	Dollars invested in chartering training programs per person per year
		Number of training programs completed per year
	Software applications	Dollars invested in new chartering software applications per year
		Number of new chartering IT improvements per year

Finally, the ability of the chartering department to keep abreast of technological innovations in the field can be measured by the number of new chartering software and chartering IT improvements per year and the invested sums in new chartering software applications. The KPI measures the ability of the company to adopt new IT systems during a time period of one year.

Based on the previous discussion Table 8.7 illustrates that possible goals and KPIs of the chartering department from a learning and growth perspective.

Financial management and KPIs

The role of the finance department is to plan, organize, audit and control the finances of the firms including monitoring of the fiscal activities and taxation. It is also responsible for undertaking an active role in negotiations for funding be it traditional bank financing or from alternative sources.

Efficient financial management is a key goal of the finance department and it is imperative to maintain the continuous support of all business activities. In this context the relevant department is responsible among others for strategic budgeting, cost containment, efficient cash flow management, debt servicing and credit use, proactive tax planning and compliance.

The finance department may also be involved in the appraisal of investment projects like for instance, newbuilding or second-hand ship purchases providing also relevant monitoring of such projects during their investment lifecycle. In this context it also assumes responsibility for allocating and managing cash reserves, working capital and other company assets. The role may be expanded through the work of the financial controller that may undertake research, analysis and reporting of economic and financial developments and the maintenance of relationships with banks, investment firms and financial institutions.

The accounting function entails the proper and timely preparation and publication of company accounts and financial statements as well as the preparation of budgets and responsibility for liaising with external auditors. The accounting department also manages the financial resources of the company including accounts payable and receivable (e.g. scheduling payments to suppliers, shipyards and agents) and monitors cash inflows and cash outflows. The accounting department may also oversee repayments of loans and other financial obligations to banks and financial institutions.

In this context, the department needs to develop budgets to cover the key operations activities such as a crewing budget, an operational budget, a materials/spares parts budget, IT budget and compare budgeted and actual transactions. A master budget serves as planning and control tool to the management since they can plan the business activities during a period.

The accounting department is also responsible for cost containment by monitoring purchasing and invoicing, stock control, developing cash management procedures and monitoring cash to cash cycle time.

On this basis possible KPIs that can be used to measure the goals of the accounting and finance department could be as shown in Table 8.8.

Table 8.8 Examples of KPIs for Accounting and Finance Department

Perspective	Strategy goal	KPIs
Shareholder value	Profit	Gross profit
		Gross profit margin
		Cash dividends paid
		Earnings before interest and taxes (EBIT)
		Earnings before interest, taxes, depreciation (EBITDA)
		Economic value added (EVA)
		Share price
		Net income
	Sales	Sales growth
		Market share gain comparison percentage
		Total sales
	Cash flow	Cash flow
		Cash flow return in investments (CFROI)
		Net change in cash
	Investment appraisal	Cash flow return on investments (CFROI)
		Return on capital employed (ROCE)
		Internal rate of return (IRR)
		Net present value (NPV)

DEPARTMENT PERFORMANCE IN SHIPPING AND TRANSPORTATION

Perspective	Strategy goal	KPIs
	Costs	Fixed costs
		Indirect costs
		Invoice processing costs
		Direct cost
		Variable costs
		Cost of goods sold (COGS)
		Accounting costs
	Expenses	Actual expenses
		Capital expenditures in dollars
		Expense account credit transactions
		Expense account debit transactions
		Expense account transactions
	Creditors	Creditor days
		Cash conversion cycle
		Accounts payable turnover
		Total payables
Internal process	Time	Budget creation cycle time
		Internal audit cycle time
		Cycle time to process payroll
		Cycle time for expense reimbursements
		Cycle time to resolve payroll errors
		Cycle time to resolve an invoice error
		Days sales outstanding
		Accounts receivable (days)
	Errors	Payment errors as a percentage of total payroll disbursement
		Percentage accuracy of financial reports
		Percentage of invoices being queried
	Debtors	Cash conversion cycle
		Debtor days
		Average monetary value of overdue invoices
		Average customer receivable
		Accounts receivable (average value)
		Accounts payable Amount due (per customer)
		Past-due receivables
		Open receivables
		Current receivables
		Receivables turnover
		Open receivables amount (per customer)
		Number of invoices outstanding
	Budget	Budgeted expenses
		Budget variance for each key metric

Quality and safety management

Safety and quality which is about continuous improvement nowadays is an integral part of the operations in the maritime industry. The achievement of relevant safety and quality related certification such as the ISM Code certification as well as the maintenance of certificates by ensuring independently audited operational procedures and equipment is an integral function of this department.

With respect to safety the relevant department aims to fulfil ship operations in a safe way that will result in zero accidents and minimal environmental impact. In this context the department needs to ensure compliance with health, safety, security and environmental laws, rules and regulations of a national and international nature.

The department plans and authorizes vessels' safety inspections by classification societies and flag authorities. The department should aim to achieve certification for non-maritime quality standards (ISO 9001 Quality Standard, ISO14001 Environmental Management System, ISO50001 Energy Management System, BS OHSAS 18001 Occupational Health and Safety Standard).

The department deals with quality, safety, health and the environment and needs to organize and oversee regular crew training on safety issues. Emergency response is a key part of the department. The remote working environment of the ship means that fully effective emergency response is essential when aiding the ship from the office during an emergency.

It is also important to use updated and upgraded technology such as an electronic QHSE system that will be able to automatically produce regular quality and safety KPI reports fleet wide.

Based on the previous discussion, Table 8.9 illustrates that possible areas for KPIs and KPI examples for quality and safety management.

Table 8.9 Quality and Safety Department Goals and KPIs

KPI Area	KPI
Shipboard safety	Number of fire incidents
	Number of groundings
	Number of failures of critical equipment and systems
	Number of collisions
	Number of explosion incidents
	Number of PSC deficiencies
	Number of PSC inspections
	Number of PSC detentions
	Number of failures of critical equipment and systems
	Number of navigational related deficiencies
	Number of operational related deficiencies
	Number of ballast water management violations
	Number of environmental related deficiencies

DEPARTMENT PERFORMANCE IN SHIPPING AND TRANSPORTATION

KPI Area	KPI
	Number of health and safety related deficiencies
	Number of security related deficiencies
	Number of ships operated under the DOC holder
	Port state control performance
	Navigational deficiencies
	Navigational incidents
Seaworthiness	Number of conditions of class
	Number of observations during commercial inspections
	Number of commercial inspections
	Planned unavailability
	Number of non-conformities
	Number of critical equipment failures
	Number of observations per internal audit
	Number of observations from external inspections
	Number of safety observations
	Number of accidents
	Number of incidents
	Number of near misses
	Ballast water management violations
Cargo-worthiness	Number of cargo related incidents
	Number of safety observations
	Number of accidents
	Number of incidents
	Number of near misses
	Cargo related incidents
	Rejection of ship or holds/tank prior to loading
	Inability to load full agreed capacity
	Failures/underperformance of ship's cargo equipment
	Negligence by ship's crew resulting in a cargo incident
	Inadequate company and ship board procedures and practices
Personnel safety	Number of fatalities due to work injuries
	Number of fatalities due to sickness
	Number of health and safety related deficiencies
	Number of lost workday cases
	Lost time injury frequency
	Lost time sickness frequency
	Crew disciplinary frequency

(*Continued*)

Table 8.9 (Continued)

KPI Area	KPI
Inspections	Number of PSC inspections
	Number of PSC inspections resulting in zero deficiencies
	Number of PSC detentions
	Number of recorded external inspections
	Number of incident investigation and analysis
Environmental performance	Emitted mass of CO_2
	Emitted mass of NOx
	NOx efficiency
	Emitted mass of Sox
	Number of contained spills of liquid
	Number of environmental related deficiencies
	Number of oil spills
	Number of ballast water management violations
	Number of releases of substances to the environment
	Carbon Intensity Index (CII)
	Energy Efficiency Existing Ship Index (EEXI)
Navigational	Number of navigational deficiencies
	Number of navigational incidents
	Number of allisions
	Number of collisions
	Number of groundings

Purchasing and supply department

The purchasing and supply department is responsible for sourcing and managing the distribution and delivery of the fleet's requirements in equipment, spare parts, stores, lubes, paints and chemicals and any other consumables that may arise in the course of ship operation and maintenance or repairs.

The practices of purchasing and supply in shipping are centred around a modified Supply Chain Operations Reference Model that identifies six distinct management processes including planning, sourcing, scheduling, receiving and delivering, returning and enabling.

Planning is about establishing plans to align resources to demand requirements of the fleet. Sourcing involves identifying the right suppliers and initiating the purchasing process with the selected companies. Scheduling is organising the procurement process followed by receipt of the materials, distribution and delivery. Returning involves organizing the logistics process for making returns of materials found to be sub-standard and enabling is about managing the business within the parameters set by regulations, risk and contractual commitments.

In the context of performing the procurement and purchasing processes the supply chain must reach performance targets relating to such goals as reliability, responsiveness, flexibility, cost and inventory and asset management and the performance attributes must be documented, measured and improved.

The department will need a systematic approach to efficiently evaluate purchasing performance. Performance is normally evaluated by considering the effectiveness and efficiency of purchasing. Purchasing efficiency is measured by considering the administrative costs of the purchasing process, in other words focusing on how well the purchasing department has performed the purchasing function and not necessarily the costs of the materials procured. If the department is using funds over and above the budget, then the purchasing function is not as efficient as planned.

On the other hand, the ability to achieve effectiveness in purchasing hinges on the cost of the procured materials in relation to market prices. The price paid for an item is not necessarily a measure of true effectiveness as processes vary depending on market conditions. A measure to assess purchasing effectiveness is the inventory turnover ratio. The ratio measures the number of times, on average, that the inventory is used (or turned over) during a period.

In measuring the performance of a procurement or supply chain system, a department may consider typical supply chain performance attributes such as supply chain reliability, responsiveness, flexibility, supply chain costs and supply chain asset management. Supply chain reliability is the performance of the supply chain in delivering the right product to the right place and the right customer at the right time in the correct condition, quantity and right packaging, with the right documentation. A typical metric or KPI would be 'perfect order fulfilment'. Supply chain responsiveness is the speed at which a supply chain procures the items to the destination. It can be measured using the 'order fulfilment cycle time'. Supply chain flexibility refers to the agility of a supply chain in responding to marketplace changes in order to gain or maintain a competitive advantage. It includes metrics such as 'upside supply chain flexibility', 'upside supply chain adaptability', 'downside supply chain adaptability'. Supply chain costs are the costs associated with operating the supply chain and can be measured using the KPIs 'cost of goods sold' or 'supply chain management costs'. Supply asset management refers to the effectiveness of the department in managing its fixed and working capital assets in order to achieve customer satisfaction. Typical metrics are 'cash to cash cycle time', 'return in supply chain fixed assets' and 'return on working capital'.

In procurement and purchasing it is important to consider best practices so as to develop the appropriate goals for the department. The department should operate with a centralized electronic purchasing system so that communication with suppliers and partners is established electronically using a simplified process (e-marketplace). Strategic sourcing must be used which involves identification of the right suppliers (sourcing) and an efficient purchasing process that involves planning fleet-wide purchasing. Strategic supplier development involves comparing suppliers, choosing the right suppliers and the right number of suppliers, engage in supplier negotiations, have dedicated expert personnel on the different product categories (electrical equipment, safety equipment etc.) to deal with the suppliers.

A purchasing department should incorporate cost saving KPIs to monitor the cost of purchases (total sum or managed spend) as well as cost reduction over time. Managed spend can be calculated as the sum of all spend run by an organization. It is important to compare how much is spent per supplier as a means of generating higher competition between suppliers and contributing to cost saving by using benchmarking and comparing supplier participation rate results.

In a purchasing department it is important to monitor the quality of the products purchased in association with other departments via cross-department collaboration. Products or consumables of low quality would affect the company's reputation and add to costs. Quality KPIs in purchasing include metrics such as percentage of rejections and disruptions due to low quality.

Delivery KPIs are required to monitor strategies that improve delivery and ensure continuity of supply. Late or early deliveries may have an impact on operational and inventory costs. The right quantity of the right type of products needs to be supplied on time. Relevant KPIs are the delivery in full on time rate (DIFOT rate) that is commonly used in logistics as well as supplier lead time, and late deliveries monitoring among others shown in Table 8.10.

Table 8.10 Purchasing Department Goals and KPIs

Strategy goal	KPIs
Strategic supplier selection	Percentage of suppliers accounting for 80% of total spend
	Number of quotations issued per year
	Number of quotations issued per product
	Weighting sustainability criteria (human rights adherence, child labour abolition, environmental protection, society impact) while choosing suppliers
	Number of suppliers on 'approved vendors' list for spares parts (quality terms)
	Supplier defect rate
Price to client	Inventory turnover rate
	Price comparisons variation

DEPARTMENT PERFORMANCE IN SHIPPING AND TRANSPORTATION

Strategy goal	KPIs
Cost-effectiveness	Percentage of managed spend against total spend on purchases
	Inventory costs
	Percentage variance to expense budget
	Cost variance levels
	Number of quotations issued per year
	Actual purchasing price – lowest price quoted (cost avoidance)
	Actual purchasing price – last price paid (cost-saving/discount)
	Adjustment of supplied quantities according to market and voyage trade patterns
Quality	Percentage of rejections
	Number of disruptions due to low quality
	Number of inaccuracies in purchasing orders
Delivery	Number of late deliveries
	Percentage delivered on schedule
	DIFOT
	Percentage of erroneous delivery over the total number of purchase orders
	Supplier lead time = Delivery time (Goods and receipts delivery) – Order time (PO acceptance)
Cycle time	Procurement cycle time
Supplier responsiveness	Number of supplier delays
	On board stock turnover for critical spare parts for main engine, auxiliary engines
	Spares urgent requisition lifecycle = PO cycle time
	Average supplier response time

Marketing and business development department

In terms of business development and marketing, the aim of the department would be to ensure that investment in marketing and business development activities and campaigns are met with an adequate return with marked contribution to sales and profitability. This department may also be tasked with building and strengthening the brand of the organization ensuring that brand value is enhanced. The aforementioned together with marketing department cost optimization would be of interest at the shareholder level. At the customer level the department is responsible for overseeing the improvement in customer attraction, customer retention and customer satisfaction, as well as the development of customer relationships and customer loyalty. To achieve such customer-related goals, the department must ensure that the right processes are in place. These include market survey processes, new service development processes and service quality measurement and brand value management processes as well as processes to ensure responsiveness to customer requirements. The human and technological resources required to achieve the aforementioned aim must also be in place.

Table 8.11 illustrates possible strategy goals and KPIs of the relevant department.

Table 8.11 Marketing Department Goals and KPIs

Strategy goal	*KPIs*
Brand value	Brand asset valuator score
	Awareness stage KPIs: brand recall index, number of social mentions per period
	Consideration stage KPIs: purchase intent, awareness to demand ratio
	Decision stage KPIs: cost per acquisition, goal conversion rate
	Delight stage KPIs: net promoter score
Marketing campaign contribution to sales or profit	Marketing cost to sales
	Marketing cost to profit
	Sales revenue: total sales to total revenue from customer acquired through marketing campaigns
	Revenue churn: revenue lost from existing customers
	MRR growth rate: monthly recurring revenue
	Sales growth
	Sales target
	Return on Marketing Investment (ROI)
Optimize marketing costs	Reduction in marketing costs
	Marketing costs v revenue
	Change in marketing costs
	Customer acquisition cot
	Cost per lead
	Cost per sale
	Marketing budget awareness-demand ratio
Client satisfaction	Client satisfaction rates
	CSAT: Customer satisfaction score
	Customer Churn Rate (CCR)
	Service Quality Level (SERVQUAL score): Reliability, Responsiveness, Assurance, Empathy Tangibles
	Customer Effort Score: feedback on the customer experience

DEPARTMENT PERFORMANCE IN SHIPPING AND TRANSPORTATION

Strategy goal	KPIs
Client attraction	Number of new clients in time-period t
	Percentage client attraction
	Average sales from new clients
	Customer acquisition rate
	Sales targets
	Sales growth
	Goal conversion rate
	Average time to conversion
Client retention	Percentage client retention
	Customer churn rate
	Percentage customer retention
	Net retention rate
	Growth in customer buying frequency
Client relationship/ loyalty	Average sales from old customer
	Customer lifetime value
	Upsell rates: increase in revenue from new customers
	Cross-sell rates: percentage revenue from current customers
	Net retention rate
Market surveys processes	Number of market surveys per time-period
	Number of staff within the intelligence generation team
	Annual budget compared to competitor
	Number of annual surveys
	Survey results generation time
New service development processes	Number of new service development processes
	Funds spent on innovation
	Time to market
	Number of innovative initiatives that became successful per period
	Revenue generated by innovations
Customer responsiveness	Number of delays
	Average time to respond to customer enquiry
	Number of delays
	First call resolution
	Number of issues
Improve staff skills	Number of training courses attended
	Investment in training per employee

(*Continued*)

Table 8.11 (Continued)

Strategy goal	KPIs
Improve marketing personnel retention rate	Retention rate of marketing personnel
	Marketing personnel attrition rate
	Overall turnover rate
Use of technology for marketing	Number of new marketing applications
	Amount invested in new marketing technology
	Return on digital investment (e.g. new marketing or sales platform)
	Percentage of AI enabled business (measures digital transformation)
	IT spent versus planned

Other departments

The insurance and claims department is responsible for taking out insurance on the ships, the crew members and depending on the type of shipping business, the cargoes. The process of taking out insurance for a marine adventure requires scrutiny of the insurance policies and the contractual clauses. The department may also be responsible for claims that arise in the course of performing shipping operations and may include hull and machinery claims, protection and indemnity claims, cargo claims stevedoring damages, stowaways, injuries, accidents, etc.

Furthermore, it is responsible for advising the top management about the annual insurance costs per vessel and per fleet, keeping the other departments up to date about the effects of possible moves that may not be covered by insurance. These include finding evidence and closely monitoring the relevant developments. For this purpose, it is in close cooperation with all the other departments and especially the technical and operations departments, as well as with the legal offices and P&I clubs. Relevant KPIs for the insurance department may include type of claims, level of claims and time for resolution or payments to be made.

The IT department fulfils an important support function in the shipping organization. It is responsible for finding, evaluating, and introducing modern tools and technological developments across the company to ensure that the company's operational objectives are efficient and effective. It is responsible for ensuring seamless internal and external communication and storage, processes and dissemination of relevant information as well as for maintaining and upgrading computer-related equipment for shore and on-board operations and provide user support. On the basis of these functions, relevant KPIs may be developed.

KPIs for transportation and warehousing

Transportation, logistics and warehousing are essential parts of the services provided by the shipping industry. The KPIs that can be used in the context of logistics and transportation can be classified into the Balanced Scorecard perspectives and in accordance with the goals that are targeted in relation to the specific functions undertaken. In this context KPIs may be financial, cost and sales related, operational, time-related, delivery-related and utilization-related. Table 8.12 provides a non-exhaustive list of such KPIs that can be used at an operational level in the transportation industries.

Table 8.12 KPIs for the Transportation and Warehousing Industry

Strategy goal area	*KPI*
Financial	Actual revenue
	Planned versus actual revenue
	Actual costs
	Planned versus actual costs
	Planned versus actual margin percentage
	Planned margin/planned revenue
	Cumulative annual growth rate (CAGR)
	Number of past-due loans
	Operating leverage
Sales related	Booked order value
	Book to ship days
	Book to fulfil ratio
	Value of open, not yet fulfilled, booked order lines
	Booked order value/fulfilled value
Inventory related	Inventory months of supply
	Planned inventory turns
	Annualized inventory turns
	Inventory turnover
	Inventory value
	Planned cost of goods sold/planned inventory value
Cost related	Annualized cost of goods sold (COGS)/average daily inventory value
	Claims percentage for freight costs
	Cost pre-carriage
	Costs on-carriage
	Vessel transport costs
	Voyage costs
	Operating costs
	Bunker costs
	Fuel consumption

(*Continued*)

Table 8.12 (Continued)

Strategy goal area	KPI
Time related	Time elapsed from pick release to ship confirm
	Time elapsed from receipt
	Transit time
	On-time pickups
	On-time line count
	Customer order promised cycle time
	Pick release to ship
	Lead time
	Lead time reliability
	Lead time variability
	Turnaround time
	Vessel transport time
	Average cycle time
	Berth time
	Waiting/queuing time
	Service frequency
	On-time performance
	Order fulfilment cycle time (OFCT) – source make and deliver
	Delivery in Full on Time (DIFOT rate)
Delivery related	Backlog value average of shipped date – firm date
	Defects per million opportunities
	Pick exceptions rate
	Planned margin
	Planned on-time shipment
	Planned service level (percentage of shipments shipped on time)
	Value of work-in-process (WIP) completions into inventory
	Production to plan rate
Utilization related	Planned resource utilization
	Planned resource usage
	Production standard value/planned standard value
	Warehouse capacity
	Average storage time
	Storage time variance
	Capacity utilization rate
	Load factor

Performance monitoring in shipping using AIS data

The evolution of big data collection using Automatic Identification Systems (AIS) and analysis techniques and the technology that supports automatic collection of data opens up the aspect of operational performance monitoring in shipping to wider new horizons. AIS provides the opportunity to record shipping and ship operating activities in real time, to store the data and enable their analysis. Various applications of AIS data have been considered for application in the shipping domain including the construction of ships, avoidance of collisions, ship emission inventory, oil spill risk assessment and green policy evaluation. AIS data is also used to evaluate the performance of ships. Factors involved in evaluating ship performance include ship utilization, speed, consumption and voyage cost.

Bibliography

Adland, R., and Jia, H. (2018). Dynamic speed choice in bulk shipping. *Maritime Economics & Logistics*, 20(2), pp. 253–266.

Adland, R., Jia, H., and Strandenes, S. P. (2017). Are AIS-based trade volume estimates reliable? The case of crude oil exports. *Maritime Policy & Management*, 44(5), pp. 657–665.

Alexandrou, S. E., Panayides, Ph. M., Tsouknidis, D. A., and Alexandrou, A. E. (2022). Green supply chain management strategy and financial performance in the shipping industry. *Maritime Policy & Management*, 49(3), pp. 376–395.

Darousos, E. F., Mejia, M. Q., and Visvikis, I. D. (2019). Sustainability, maritime governance, and business performance in a self-regulated shipping industry: A study on the BIMCO shipping KPI standard. In Panayides, Ph. M. (ed) *The Routledge Handbook of Maritime Management*. London: Routledge.

Eide, M. S., Endresen, Ø., Breivik, Ø., Brude, O. W., Ellingsen, I. H., Røang, K., and Brett, P. O. (2007). Prevention of oil spill from shipping by modelling of dynamic risk. *Marine Pollution Bulletin*, 54(10), pp. 1619–1633.

Furnival, D., and Crispe, J. (2017). Technical operations management. In Visvikis, I., and Panayides, Ph. M. (eds) *Shipping Operations Management Chapter*, pp. 99–128. Malmo: WMU Studies in Maritime Affairs.

Jia, H., Adland, R., Prakash, V., and Smith, T. (2017). Energy efficiency with the application of virtual arrival policy. *Transportation Research Part D: Transport and Environment*, 54, pp. 50–60.

Lagoudis, I. N., Lalwani, C. S., and Naim, M. (2006). Ranking of factors contributing to higher performance in the ocean transportation industry: A multiattribute utility theory approach. *Maritime Policy & Management*, 33(4), pp. 345–369.

Otheitis, N., and Kunc, M. (2015). Performance measurement adoption and business performance: An exploratory study in the shipping industry. *Management Decision*, 53(1), pp. 139–159.

Winther, M., Christensen, J. H., Plejdrup, M. S., Ravn, E. S., Eriksson, Ó. F., and Kristensen, H. O. (2014). Emission inventories for ships in the arctic based on satellite sampled AIS data. *Atmospheric Environment*, 91, pp. 1–14.

Yang, D., Wu, L., Wang, S., Jia, H., and Li, K. X. (2019). How big data enriches maritime research – A critical review of Automatic Identification System (AIS) data applications. *Transport Reviews*, 39(6), pp. 755–773.

CHAPTER 9

Implementation, data analytics and shipping KPI reporting systems

Introduction

This chapter will describe the process for implementing a performance management system based on the balanced scorecard in a maritime context and highlight the characteristics of software and automation solutions that need to be adopted for correct implementation.

Implementation of the performance management system

Implementing a balanced scorecard performance management system requires a project manager and commitment from the top. Senior management commitment and quick implementation are critical for success. It is also important to involve individuals from all business units, department and teams. Employees need incentives and recognition to embark on the transformation journey.

The implementation journey requires investment to institute the necessary motivation as well as achieve recognition. Employees will inevitably respond to recognition for the achievement of KPIs as well as to bonus pools for reaching or exceeding targeted performance. It is important to achieve a balance between monetary and non-monetary incentives to achieve the desired behaviours.

Implementation also requires investment in automation and analytics. Detailed analytics can assist management to translate corporate strategy to operational terms and recognize the financial impact of corporate strategy.

The expected time for developing the corporate balanced scorecard is 3–4 weeks and this will incorporate meetings and workshops. The expected time for cascading the balanced scorecard to one level is 4–5 weeks (meetings and 3–4 workshops). Significant part of the development is done by the project team. These estimates are based on a medium-sized organization with project team members that, facilitate meetings, synthesize inputs and confirm design through workshops.

For a company with an operations focused KPI scorecard, the following process will be implemented:

1. Review strategy and set corporate level objectives
2. Develop operational objectives and cascade to departments

124

DOI: 10.4324/9781315717845-9

3. Develop links of KPIs to objectives and discontinue any non-important KPIs
4. Set targets and align the organization, processes and intangible assets

The work plan is illustrated in Table 9.1

A project manager should be appointed that will lead initiatives, coordinate activities, organize the meetings, run workshops and contribute to scorecard development. To ensure the involvement of all departments, it is important that a person is appointed to represent each business unit or department and assist with workshops and meetings, work on business unit/department scorecard development and procure the necessary data from the business unit/department.

The balanced scorecard management system is dynamic and needs management. It is imperative to ensure that strategy updates are incorporated into the balanced scorecard system, that the balanced scorecard is linked to budgets and that the measurement process is accurate, valid, reliable and data collection is synchronized. The system should be able to produce reports that facilitate decision

Table 9.1 Work Plan for Performance Management System Implementation

Steps	*Activities*	*Expected duration*
Project planning	Design phases, form team, kick-off project	2 weeks
Mapping strategy	Review strategy	2 weeks
	Develop and finalize maps	
Corporate balanced scorecard	Meeting with stakeholders	4 weeks
	Run workshops with managers to confirm first draft	
	Meeting for clarifications and receiving agreement	
Unit balanced scorecards	Meeting with stakeholders	6 weeks
	Run workshops with managers to confirm first draft	
	Meeting for clarifications and receiving agreement	
Measurement	Measurement gaps are identified, and action plans are developed	2 weeks
	Initiatives are identified	
Reporting	Management information is received, and new reports are created	2 weeks
	Automation gaps are identified, and action plans are developed	
Support processes	Appraisal process is reviewed	2 weeks
	A communications system is developed	

making, link individual staff goals and KPIs to the balanced scorecard and ensure that the right messages are communicated to staff. Staff need to understand strategy and be trained and incentivized to execute strategy. For the achievement of that mentioned before, it is imperative that technology is required to institutionalize the balanced scorecard measurement and management system.

Automation and technology

The balanced scorecard measurement and management system is multi-dimensional, and cascading makes it rather complex to manage. Challenges include the timely collection of data through the integration of the numerous data sources. Efficiency and effectiveness can be achieved through automation. The system should adhere to some characteristics for ideal functionality including the ability to assist the user in:

- Creating scorecards
- Creating strategy maps
- Cascading and linking scorecards
- Uploading and analyzing data from company databases
- Utilizing business intelligence and presentation tools
- Importing market data for benchmarking purposes
- Tracking initiatives
- Undertaking risk management

In addition, the software system should have a client friendly interface, communication tools and a personalized portal.

In terms of the KPI set the capabilities of the software system should include the ability to churn out metric variables bearing in mind the depth of measures that exist in the maritime industry (there is a multitude of managerial, operational and ship level data). Beyond KPI depth, the software should be easy to understand and use in the dashboard and reporting system and be interactive with data updates in real time and in synchronization across multiple access points. If one user makes a specific change to the dataset, others should be kept in the loop and be informed immediately. The platform should allow multiple users to source from the same dataset in real time so that any data preparation time can be minimized. The software should be able to convey actionable business intelligence through the use of graphics and visuals including line charts, pie charts, graphs and Gantt charts. Finally, drag and drop tools are a necessity in a software of this nature.

The automation solution called for should have the ability to collect and integrate data from various sources in the organization including from existing software systems. This includes, accounting, finance, operations, crewing, the ship itself and other internal and external sources. The system should be able to collect, store, aggregate and analyse the data and produce dashboards that are useful to decision makers and reports that are comprehensive and useable by those responsible. Information and results need to reach the end user in a timely and useable format to facilitate quick decision making. To achieve this, any software solution should include visuals such as dashboards and graphics and allow the production of comprehensive reports. The software should have analytics capabilities and allow drilldown and sharing.

Users are bound to benefit more from software that adheres to the following characteristics:

- Has storage and database capabilities
- Offers controlled access
- Enables regular back-up
- Prevents human manipulation of data
- Enables time saving and data driven report generation
- Preserves historical data and allows for trend analysis
- Facilitates dimensional modelling
- Develops hierarchies based on business requirements
- Provides an environment for business exploration of data such as company structure, assets, deficiencies and other useful information
- Allows for drill and dice capabilities with the visualization objects
- Is customisable.

The system can potentially provide benefits to the IT department including the reduction of requests for reports from users, integration of operational systems into a single data warehouse, ease for data consolidation and higher automation saving time and effort to develop, produce and dispatch reports and information.

It is also advisable for companies in the maritime domain to move beyond the adoption of automation for managing and measuring performance towards the implementation of a more dynamic system that will enable the collection of continuous big data and enable in-depth analysis of operational and strategic performance by adoption of advanced analytics to discover deeper insights, make predictions and generate suggestions. Such techniques include data/text mining, machine learning, simulation, neural networks, forecasting and visualization, multivariate analysis and complex event processing among others.

The possible use of cloud technology where different servers, storage and applications can be delivered to the company's computers and other devices provides endless opportunities for maritime companies. On the other hand, advanced analytics techniques create data driven insights that will enable managers to take proactive action in the effort to maximize operational efficiency and optimize revenue and costs. In the maritime domain advanced analytics may enable voyage optimization, just-in-time delivery of spare parts, crew and bunkers, improvement in equipment and engine reliability to name but a few applications. Analytics can also target issues such as vessel utilization and deployment (e.g. in a liner service), terminal productivity through reduction of bottlenecks through ship arrival and departure optimization, bunker fuel optimization (speed profile of vessel) and market intelligence and forecasts. Benefits include the reduction of failures, lower risk exposure, optimization of labour, asset deployment and operations and ultimately customer satisfaction and loyalty. Automatic identification system (AIS) data can also be used to derive and use big data.

Reports and deliverables

A performance management system will yield several deliverables for use by the relevant people in the organization, including KPI reports, scorecards, presentations and dashboards. These tools may be used to track progress against targets and goals and to facilitate decision making and improve performance.

Maritime companies produce enormous amounts of data. They include data on operations, crewing, chartering, HSEQ, purchasing, ship performance and data about customers, charterers, brokers, markets, financial, accounting, regulatory compliance, etc. The data can be classified into critical or important. Some data may not be relevant.

A KPI report represents a business performance tool that effectively visualizes KPIs. Such reports should typically contain a mixture of charts, graphs and tabular information that is critical. A report focuses on an analytical interpretation of the underlying measures, using trend graphs and tabular formats to support the decision-making process of managers.

Reports allow the users to slice through the data and facilitate summarizing of the information so it is more manageable, and ultimately more usable. A KPI report is not only a more refined way to collate this data, but they are also designed to visualize KPIs and metrics that specifically target performance against objectives. They are the pinnacle of a structured performance monitoring or improvement process.

Monitoring is performed through dashboard visuals. For example, if the level of customer satisfaction is less than its target, then a red signal icon can be programmed to be displayed on the dashboard.

Conclusion

The focus of this book has been to provide a strategic approach to the measurement of performance in the shipping industry and in doing so to highlight a variety of KPIs that may be relevant to the measurement and management of performance at corporate and departmental level in shipping.

In accordance with relevant literature, the Balanced Scorecard approach can have significant benefits to a company and can actually lead to improved performance compared to the use of other traditional performances measurement systems. By taking a balanced approach to performance measurement, companies have the opportunity to incorporate diverse metrics of critical success factor areas to ensure that performance is measured holistically and comprehensively. It also provides opportunities to develop new and innovative KPIs. The approach not only utilizes the traditional financial performance measures but also incorporates others in the evolving business context even beyond the traditional Balanced

Scorecard perspective of customer, internal processes and learning and growth. For example, the shipping industry nowadays is focused on the issues of sustainability, environmental, social and ethical concepts and the Balanced Scorecard approach readily provides the opportunity to incorporate relevant goals and KPIs and monitor and manage performance along these dimensions.

Bibliography

Aliakbari Nouri, F., Shafiei Nikabadi, M., and Olfat, L. (2019). Developing the framework of sustainable service supply chain balanced scorecard (SSSC BSC). *International Journal of Productivity and Performance Management*, 68(1), pp. 148–170.

Asiaei, K., and Bontis, N. (2019). Using a balanced scorecard to manage corporate social responsibility. *Knowledge and Process Management*, 26(4), pp. 371–379.

Atikno, W., Setiawan, I., and Taufik, D. A. (2021). Key performance indicators implementation: Literature review and development for performance measurement. *IJIEM-Indonesian Journal of Industrial Engineering and Management*, 2(3), pp. 189–197.

Davis, S., and Albright, T. (2004). An investigation of the effect of balanced scorecard implementation on financial performance. *Management Accounting Research*, 15(2), pp. 135–153.

Hassini, E., Surti, C., and Searcy, C. (2012). A literature review and a case study of sustainable supply chains with a focus on metrics. *International Journal of Production Economics*, 140(1), pp. 69–82.

Lueg, R., and Vu, L. (2015). Success factors in balanced scorecard implementations – A literature review. *Management Revue*, pp. 306–327.

Quesado, P. R., Aibar Guzmán, B., and Lima Rodrigues, L. (2018). Advantages and contributions in the balanced scorecard implementation. *Intangible Capital*, 14(1), pp. 186–201.

Setiawan, I., and Purba, H. H. (2020). A systematic literature review of key performance indicators (KPIs) implementation. *Journal of Industrial Engineering & Management Research*, 1(3), pp. 200–208.

INDEX

Note: Page numbers in **bold** indicate a table on the corresponding page.

action plans 51
automation 126–128

Balanced Scorecard 19–21; implementing 21–23
bulk logistics goals 36–37
business development department 117–120, **118–120**
business strategy 25–28, 31–33; company vision 28; formulation 28; identifying goals 36–40; mission and core values 28–29; ship managers generic strategy map models 34–35; shipowners' generic strategy map models 33–34; strategic goals 30–31; value proposition 29–30

cascation process 93
case studies 62; containership charter owner 74–78; dry bulk shipping company 62–65, 87–89; liner shipping company 65–71; logistics service provider 82–87; tanker company 71–73; third-party ship management 78–82
chartering department: objectives and KPIs 100–109, **102**, **106**, **108–109**
chartering goals 39–40
commercial management goals 39–40
companies *see* case studies
company vision 28
container charter owner 74–78, **77–78**
container shipping goals 37–38
core values 28–29
corporate KPIs 49–50, 53–60, **60**
corporate strategy 26
crewing department: objectives and KPIs 97–100, **98–100**

crewing goals 39; chartering department 104–105
customer KPIs 55–58, **57**
customer perspective: ship manager 35; shipowners' 33
customer value 13

data analytics 124–129
deliverables 128
departmental KPIs 49–50; developing 93
departmental objectives: chartering department 100–109, **102**, **106**, **108–109**; crewing department 97–100, **98–100**; developing 93; operations department 94, **94–95**; technical department 95–97, **96–97**
department performance: AIS data 122–123; cascation process 93; chartering department 100–109, **102**, **106**, **108–109**; crewing department 97–100, **98–100**; financial management 109–111, **110–111**; marketing and business development department 117–120, **118–120**; operations department 94–95, **94–95**; other departments 120; purchasing and supply department 114–117, **116–117**; quality and safety management 112–114, **112–114**; technical department 95–97, **96–97**; transportation and warehousing 121–122, **121–122**; typical departments and functions 91–92
dry bulk shipping company 62–65, 87–89, **88–89**

economic performance 3–4
environmental performance 4–5

131

INDEX

financial goals 13; chartering department 102–104

financial KPIs 53–55, **54**

financial management 109–111, **110–111**

financial management goals 40

financial performance 3–4

financial performance measurement 16–17

financial perspective: ship manager 35; shipowners' 33

functions in maritime organizations 91–92

goals 12–14; identifying 36–40; strategic 30–31

governance-related performance 6

growth values: chartering department 108–109

growth perspective *see* learning and growth perspective

implementation 124–129

initiatives 51

innovation: chartering department 108–109; and goals 14

internal process goals: chartering department 105–107

internal process KPIs 58–59, **59**

internal process perspective: ship manager 35; shipowners' 34

key performance indicators (KPIs) 10–11, 43–51, 53–60, **60**, 124–129; chartering department 100–109, **102**, **106**, **108–109**; container charter owner 74–76; crewing department 97–100, **98–100**; departmental 93; dry bulk shipping company 64–65, 87–88; financial management 109–111, **110–111**; liner shipping company 67–68; logistics service provider 83–87; operations department 94, **94–95**; tanker company 72; technical department 95–97, **96–97**; third-party ship management 79; transportation and warehousing 121–122, **121–122**

learning: chartering department 108–109; and goals 14

learning and growth KPIs 59–60, **60**

learning and growth perspective: ship manager 35; shipowners' 34

liner shipping company 65–71, **66–67**, **69–71**

logistics service provider 82–87, **85–86**

management *see* performance management

Management and Self-Assessment (MSA) programme 12

managers *see* ship managers

mapping 25–28, 31–33; company vision 28; identifying goals 36–40; mission and core values 28–29; scope of strategy maps 31; ship managers generic strategy map models 34–35; shipowners' generic strategy map models 33–34; strategic goals/objectives 30–32; value proposition 29–30

marketing department 117–120, **118–120**

measurement *see* performance measurement

mission 28–29; container charter owner 74; dry bulk shipping company 62–63, 87; liner shipping company 67; logistics service provider 83

objectives *see* departmental objectives; strategic objectives

operational performance 5–6

operations: goals to create value through 14

operations department: objectives and KPIs 94, **94–95**

operations management: approaches 17–18

organizational approaches 18–19

people 18–19

performance *see* department performance; key performance indicators; performance indicators; performance management; performance management system; performance measurement

performance indicators 10

performance management 1–2, 9–14; need for 2–6

performance management system 16–23; implementation of 124–126, **125**

performance measurement 1–2; approaches to 16–19; frequency of measuring KPIs 49

procurement goals 40

purchasing and supply department 114–117, **116–117**

purchasing goals 40

quality goals 40

quality management 112–114, **112–114**

reporting systems 124–129

reports 128

resources 14

safety management 112–114, **112–114**
safety management goals 40
ship managers: generic strategy map
   models 34–35
ship operations management goals 38–39
shipowners: generic strategy map models
   33–34
shipping, department performance in: AIS
   data 122–123; cascation process 93;
   chartering department 100–109, **102**,
   106, **108–109**; crewing department
   97–100, **98–100**; financial management
   109–111, **110–111**; marketing and
   business development department
   117–120, **118–120**; operations
   department 94–95, **94–95**; other
   departments 120; purchasing and supply
   department 114–117, **116–117**; quality
   and safety management 112–114,
   112–114; technical department 95–97,
   96–97; transportation and warehousing
   121–122, **121–122**; typical departments
   and functions 91–92
Shipping KPI Standard Project 10–12
Shipping Performance Indexes 11
social performance 6
strategic goals 30–31
strategic objectives, mapping of 31–32
strategy 16–19, 25–28; container charter
   owner 74–76; dry bulk shipping
   company 64–65, 87–88; liner shipping
   company 67–68; logistics service
   provider 83–87; tanker company 72;
   third-party ship management 79;
   see also business strategy; strategic
   objectives; strategy goals; strategy maps
strategy goals: dry bulk shipping company 63
strategy maps 31; development 32–33;
   ship managers generic strategy map
   models 34–35; shipowners' generic
   strategy map models 33–34

supply *see* purchasing and supply
   department

tanker company 71–73, **72–73**
technical department: objectives and KPIs
   95–97, **96–97**
technical management goals 39
technology: and automation 126–128; and
   goals 14
third-party ship management 78–82,
   80–82
transportation, department performance
   in: AIS data 122–123; cascation
   process 93; chartering department
   100–109, **102**, **106**, **108–109**;
   crewing department 97–100, **98–100**;
   financial management 109–111,
   110–111; marketing and business
   development department 117–120,
   118–120; operations department
   94–95, **94–95**; other departments 120;
   purchasing and supply department
   114–117, **116–117**; quality and safety
   management 112–114, **112–114**;
   technical department 95–97, **96–97**;
   transportation and warehousing
   121–122, **121–122**; typical
   departments and functions 91–92

value: goals to create value through
   operations 14; *see also* customer value;
   value proposition
value proposition 29–30
values *see* core values
vision: container charter owner 74; dry
   bulk shipping company 62–63, 87;
   liner shipping company 67; logistics
   service provider 83; tanker company 71;
   see also company vision

warehousing: KPIs for 121–122, **121–122**